DEDICATION

For my wonderful family.

It couldn't happen without you.

ACKNOWLEDGMENTS

This book is due in large part to two people. First, there's my buddy Mike. Many of our conversations have turned into inspiration for me. I can't remember the exact words he said during one of our chats, but it was something along the lines of me writing a book to show what to do after the picture is taken. Mike has been in the photo finishing business for many years, so he definitely knows the benefits of image processing.

The other person who helped breathe life into this book is my editor Ted Waitt. Ted and I have had many a long chat about expanding the Snapshots series into other realms of photography. He often puts up with my ramblings, but it didn't take much for me to convince him that this was a book worth writing. It was his task to actually make it a reality, which is no small feat. His support and ability to keep me focused are very much appreciated.

Of course, Ted is not the only force behind this book. In fact, he's so busy these days that he introduced me to editor Susan Rimerman, whom it was a pleasure working with right from the start. She is no stranger to the Snapshots series, having already worked on several of the other books, and it was great having her experience at the table for this one.

Lastly, and I know this may sound kind of corny, but I want to thank you. I get emails and Web site comments all the time that offer me inspiration and guidance in knowing what it is that you want to learn. It is always a true joy and pleasure for me to help someone with their photography. It brings so much fulfillment to my life every day, and I am just thankful that so many of you have turned to me to help you with your own pursuits. It really is a great honor and pleasure to help.

Please return / renew by date shown.
You can renew at: **norlink.norfolk.gov.uk**
or by telephone: **0344 800 8006**
Please have your library card & PIN ready.

Photoshop Elements:
From
Snapshots to
Great Shots

Jeff Revell

**Peachpit
Press**

Photoshop Elements: From Snapshots to Great Shots
Jeff Revell

Peachpit Press
1249 Eighth Street
Berkeley, CA 94710
510/524-2178
510/524-2221 (fax)

Find us on the Web at www.peachpit.com
To report errors, please send a note to errata@peachpit.com
Peachpit Press is a division of Pearson Education

Editor: Susan Rimerman
Copyeditor / Proofreader: Scout Festa
Production Editor / Compositor: Danielle Foster
Indexer: James Minkin
Interior Design: Riezebos Holzbaur Design Group
Cover Design: Aren Straiger
Cover Image: Jeff Revell
Author Photo: Scott Kelby

ISBN-13   978-0-321-80831-8
ISBN-10   0-321-80831-2

9 8 7 6 5 4 3 2 1

Printed and bound in the United States of America

Contents

CHAPTER 9: FIXING PHOTOS
A Step-by-Step Look at My Editing Workflow

Introduction

I have written quite a few books in the *From Snapshots to Great Shots* series, and most of them have been about cameras. My philosophy for writing them has been to give a good foundation for taking great photographs through the application of camera technology and knowledge. It's so important to understand the fundamentals and how to apply them when taking photographs. But is that all there is to making a good image? Well, it used to be.

There was a time when all you could control was the exposure of your film, and everything else was handed off to a photofinisher. It was their job to make sure that the film was processed correctly and that everything from that point on was done to give you a decent-looking image. Just how decent depended on who was doing the processing.

Today you can still drop off your files at the local drugstore and get photos back, but if you want to get great-looking images, you need to take control of that other side of the photography coin—the image processing. That's why I wanted to write this book. Because showing you how to take a great photo is just part of the equation. To get the most from your photographic efforts, you need to learn how to finish the photo by using software tools like Adobe Photoshop Elements.

There's an old saying that goes—*Give a man a fish, feed him today. Teach a man to fish and you feed him for life.* Well, not really. You have to teach him not only how to catch it, but also how to clean it and cook it. Otherwise he just has a bunch of fish that he doesn't know what to do with. That's what we are going to do here. Now that you have caught your fish, let's clean it and cook it and make it a truly great meal.

I have hopefully given you some clue as to what this book is about, but if you still aren't sure, read the Q&A.

Q: WHY ADOBE PHOTOSHOP ELEMENTS?

A: It's true that there are a lot of image processing programs on the market to choose from, but I wanted to pick a program that had all the power to handle many different image file types, including raw and JPEG. The program also needed enhancement tools that are fairly simple to use but also very powerful. I also wanted to ensure that there would be image management as well as lots of output options. The biggest feature, though, was having a price tag that wouldn't break the bank. Photoshop Elements has all of these things and more. It has a great image management feature called the Organizer, and many of the same great tools as its big brother, Adobe Photoshop. Elements uses the Adobe Camera Raw software for complete control over raw image processing, and it has a very reasonable price tag.

Q: DOES IT MATTER IF I HAVE A MAC OR PC?

A: Nope. The program performs almost identically on either platform. When there is a difference between the keyboard shortcuts, I list the Windows shortcut first, followed by the Mac shortcut in parentheses, like this: To deselect, press Shift-Control-A (Shift-Command-A). The screen captures in this book were made on a PC using the Windows 7 operating system, so you might see some aesthetic differences (buttons, cursors, and the like), but overall the program interface should look almost identical.

Q: YOU WROTE THIS BOOK USING ELEMENTS 10, DOES THAT MEAN I CAN'T USE IT FOR MY EARLIER VERSION?

A: Not at all. Notice that there is no version number on the front of this book. That's because most of the things we are going to be doing will be general in nature and use the same tools that have been available in previous versions of Elements. I have tried to focus on the basics of image processing, so we address things like color correction, cropping, exposure adjustments, sharpening, and so on. The tools to perform these operations have changed little over the years and will still be there in future versions as well. They are the core elements of image processing, and just like f-stops and shutter speeds, they will probably change very little in the future.

Q: DO YOU COVER EVERY FEATURE?

A: Not even close. Adobe Photoshop Elements is jam-packed with hundreds of features, and this book would be many hundreds of pages long if I covered all of it. My focus for this book is to bring you the information and techniques necessary to take images from your camera and enhance them into something great. I also want you to be able to hit the ground running without getting bogged down by a lot of features.

As in my camera books, we are going to cover the tools and features that will give you a great image processing foundation and let you start improving your photos right away.

Q: WHAT CAN I EXPECT TO LEARN FROM THIS BOOK?

A: I like to think of image processing as a three-step process. First there is the import, where I move images from my camera to my computer. Next, it's time to work them over, giving them the right treatment to really fulfill the vision I had when I took the photo. The third step is to do something with my images, whether it's making prints to hang on the wall or sharing them with friends, family, or even clients. These are the processes that you will learn. They aren't overly complicated or advanced, but you don't have to tell anyone that.

Q: WHAT ARE THE ASSIGNMENTS ALL ABOUT?

A: At the end of most of the chapters, you will find short assignments where I give you some suggestions as to how you can apply the lessons of the chapter to help reinforce everything you just learned. A lot of the information covered in the chapters will be new to you, and I'm a firm believer in learning by doing. The assignments are simple exercises that will help you gain a better understanding, and also take a nice break, before moving on to the next chapter.

Q: IS THERE ANYTHING ELSE I SHOULD KNOW BEFORE GETTING STARTED?

A: I realize that not everyone out there is shooting raw image files. Since I am such a huge believer in shooting raw (see Chapter 4), I thought it would be good to give you some of my files to use so that you can follow along with the lessons in Adobe Camera Raw. To access the bonus content, create an account here: peachpit.com/elements_snapshots (it's free), then enter the book's ISBN and follow the book registration instructions. After you register the book, a link to the bonus content will be listed on your Account page next to the book title under Registered Products.

Q: IS THAT IT?

A: I also know what fun it can be to share what you learned with others and maybe even show off a bit. To that end, I invite you to show off your before and after shots in the *Elements: From Snapshots to Great Shots* Flickr group. You have worked hard learning new things, so go ahead, join the group, and show us your Great Shots. Just point your browser to www.flickr.com/groups/elements_fromsnapshotstogreatshots, and join in on the fun. I'm looking forward to seeing your work.

1

ISO 100
1/640 sec.
f/4.5
35mm lens

From Camera to Computer

IMPORTING YOUR IMAGES

This may seem like a pretty elementary place to start, but let's face it: You can't do anything to your photographs until you get them into your computer. Believe it or not, this is where things can really go wrong for a lot of people. What do I mean by that? Well, being organized is the key component to a fast and efficient workflow. By developing a plan for how and where to put your photos, you will be well on the way not only to working faster, but also to finding your photographs later on when you really want them. The first step in this process is the import.

I can't tell you how many times I have looked through someone else's computer and found images scattered about in numerous folders. If you are lucky, they might all be in the My Pictures folder, but that's not always the case. The best way to combat this is to get organized from the moment that you import your images into your computer. So let's check out the Elements Organizer and start importing some photos.

1

PORING OVER THE PICTURE

Use the flexible viewing options in the Organizer to sort and view your images.

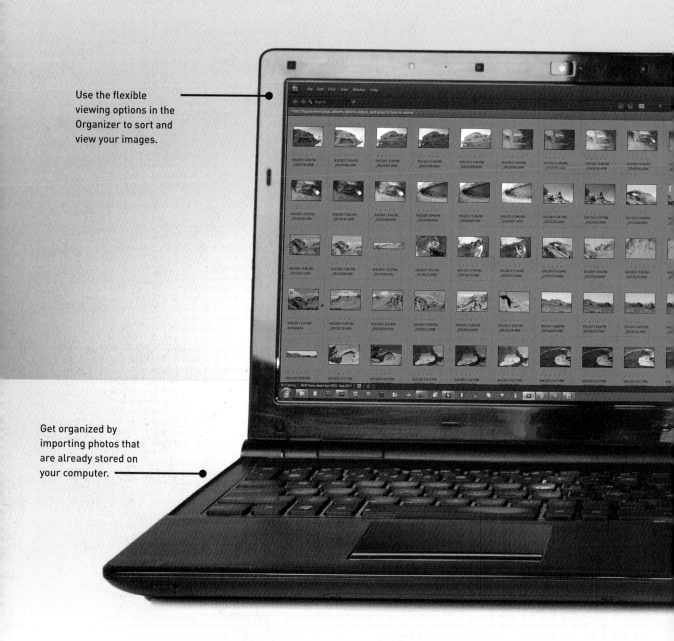

Get organized by importing photos that are already stored on your computer.

Easily import your images
to the Organizer directly
from your camera or a
card reader.

IMPORTING PHOTOS FROM YOUR CAMERA OR CARD READER

I love taking photographs. Working with my camera and accessories to capture a moment is one of my most fulfilling experiences, but what have I really done up to that point? I have captured the image on a memory card and probably looked at it on the camera's LCD screen. There's not a lot else you can do with an image while it sits there in the camera, so importing it into my computer is the logical next step.

Adobe Photoshop Elements allows you to perform this process either by connecting your camera to the computer or by removing the card from the camera and using a connected card reader. Let's start by importing pictures from our camera. To do this, you will need a USB cord, which most likely was included with your camera when you bought it.

Before attaching your camera to the computer, read your camera's manual for any specific instructions related to this procedure.

FIGURE 1.1
The Elements
Organizer interface.

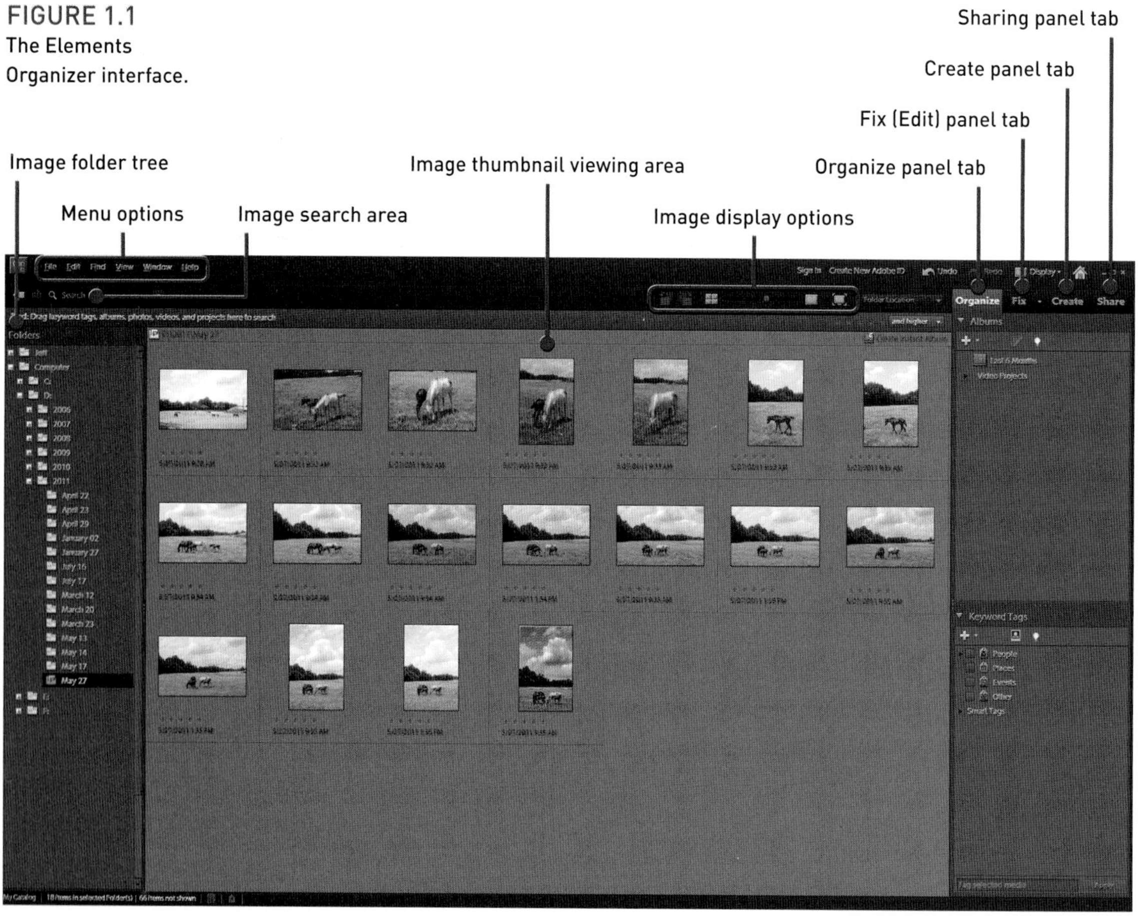

Sharing panel tab

Create panel tab

Fix (Edit) panel tab

Organize panel tab

Image folder tree

Image thumbnail viewing area

Image display options

Menu options

Image search area

After the camera is attached and turned on, open the Elements Organizer (**Figure 1.1**) and then click the File menu. Select Get Photos and Videos > From Camera or Card Reader (the keyboard shortcut for performing this action is Control-G for Windows or Command-G for Mac).

When the Photo Downloader dialog opens, you'll have to make some decisions before moving forward (**Figure 1.2**). First, you need to select your source. Select your attached camera from the Get Photos from drop-down menu. Now it's time to make some decisions about how to organize your photographs on the computer.

The Import Settings section of the dialog lets you determine folder locations, create some folders, rename your files, and select deleting options for images on the card or camera. The first thing you need to decide is what location you want your photographs to reside in on the hard drive. Typically this would be your Pictures folder, but you

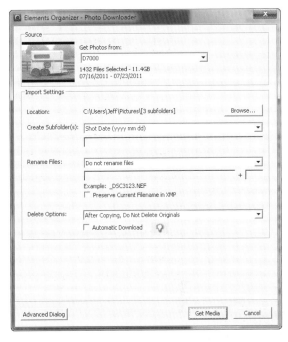

FIGURE 1.2
The Photo Downloader dialog.

may decide to use a different location, such as a second hard drive. To select a different location for your photographs, click the Browse button, navigate to the folder or drive where you would like your photos to end up, click the New Folder button, and type in the name of your new folder. Just make sure to click the new folder to select it before pressing the Select Folder button (**Figure 1.3**).

NOTE

To open the Organizer in Windows, click the Start button and then select Adobe Photoshop Elements from the All Programs section. When the opening splash screen appears, click Elements Organizer. If you are using a Mac, look in your Applications folder for the Adobe Photoshop Elements icon and click it to start the program.

FIGURE 1.3
Click the New
folder button to
create a custom
download location.

Subfolders are a nice way of allowing you to sort images by topic or date. I prefer to sort my photographs into subfolders using the date that I took the photographs. The Organizer gives you several different date options to choose from when naming a subfolder. If none of these work for you, you may create your own custom sub-folder. Simply select Custom from the drop-down menu, and then fill in the desired name in the space below.

Another option when importing is the renaming of image files. The default setting leaves the file names as they were when they were created in the camera. If you would like to change this option, simply click the down arrow and choose one of the many presets, or create your own custom naming convention.

The next option allows you to decide what to do with your images on the memory card after they have been imported. The default setting does not delete the originals but rather leaves them on the card for you to deal with later. This is the option that I prefer when importing images. It's just a personal preference, but I like to make sure all of the images are intact and then delete them in the camera when I am ready. The other two available options will delete the images off the card after copying, or after copying and verifying.

You will notice a small check box labeled Automatic Download near the bottom of the Import Settings section. If you select this check box, the Adobe Downloader will automatically start when the computer recognizes an attached camera or card reader.

Images will be downloaded using the default settings from the preferences. I prefer to leave this turned off and to instead select my import options with each session.

You will also notice an Advanced Dialog button at the bottom of the dialog. Selecting this option expands the dialog options, giving you more information and the ability to add more data during import. The advanced options will allow you to select individual images for import, apply ownership and copyright data to the images, and perform some automatic tasks such as fixing red eyes, suggesting photo stacks, and importing into an album (**Figure 1.4**).

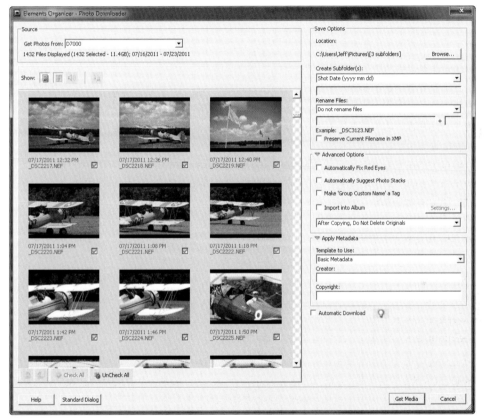

FIGURE 1.4
The Advanced Photo Downloader dialog.

After you have set all of your options in the dialog, click the Get Media button to begin the import process (**Figure 1.5**).

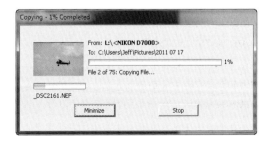

FIGURE 1.5
Once your download has begun, a progress window will keep you updated.

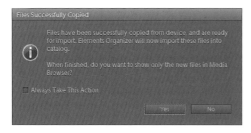

FIGURE 1.6
Click the Yes button to see only the images that were just downloaded.

This is not quite the end of the procedure. When all of your files have been moved, another box will pop up to let you know that you have successfully moved or copied your files and that they are now ready for import in the Elements Organizer catalog (**Figure 1.6**). The big question is whether you want to see only the new files in the browser or all of your images. I like to focus my attention on the newly updated images, so I select Yes. I also select the check box for making this my default setting, which means I won't ever have to see this box again.

NOTE

To make all of your images visible again in the Organizer window, simply press the Show All button at the top of the thumbnail window.

CREATING A BACKUP

Sometimes bad things happen. One day you will have a hard drive failure. It can be a devastating thing to lose all of your files, maybe even more so to lose all of your photographs. Consider creating a backup copy of your images onto a separate drive. There are many types to choose from, from a single disc to a more robust redundant drive system like the Drobo. The important thing is that you don't put off getting and using one until it's too late.

Luckily, there are some great backup options available within Elements to help protect against image loss. Under the File menu in the Organizer you will see two options. The first lets you copy or move your files to your separate backup drive. The second will back up your images along with your Organizer catalog. This is a nice option, and I highly recommend it for your peace of mind. The first time you back up your catalog, you will need to perform a full backup, but later on you can do incremental backups to keep it updated. Just follow the easy instructions in the backup dialog and you will be well on your way to some peace of mind.

I recommend that you use a backup storage device other than your computer's hard drive. An external drive or DVD is safer than using the drive in your computer because you can keep an external drive separate from your computer and safeguard it against catastrophes such as lightning strikes and power surges. Some people go as far as putting their backups in a safe deposit box.

IMPORTING FROM A CARD READER

The nice thing about importing from a card reader is that it's the same procedure that we just went through for importing directly from your camera. The only difference between the two processes is the selection of the source. For card reader imports, follow the same process that we just went over, except this time select your card reader from the Get Photos From drop-down menu. This is located in the Source section of the Photo Downloader dialog.

STEP BY STEP

Let's run through that process one more time to make sure you have it down:

1. Attach your card reader or camera to the computer.
2. Select File > Get Photos and Videos > From Camera or Card Reader.
3. Select your source from the Get Photos From drop-down menu.
4. Adjust your Import Settings options.
5. Click the Get Media button to begin the import process.

IMPORTING FROM A FOLDER

The chances are you already have photographs stored on your computer. In order to make your life a little easier, as well as to make your photos easier to find, you should add those photos to the Organizer as well. Depending on how many photographs you have stored on your computer, this might take a little while to do, but it is well worth it in the end.

THE FOLDER IMPORT PROCESS

To add photos to the Organizer, select File > Get Photos and Videos > From Files and Folders. You can also access this function by pressing Control-Shift-G (Command-Shift-G on a Mac).

From here it's just a matter of navigating to the folder where your photographs are stored and selecting the files that you want to import (**Figure 1.7**). You have the option of selecting an entire folder or individual files. If you select a top-level folder (meaning there are folders inside of it), all of the files in the subfolders will also be imported.

FIGURE 1.7
The files and
folders selection
window.

JUST WHAT IS A WORKFLOW?

Hang around enough photography Web sites and forums and you will hear the term *work-flow*. So just what is a workflow anyway? Simply put, this describes the digital photographic process and how you want to handle your images. A typical workflow might include: shooting the photos, importing and organizing the image files, sorting through the shots to find the keepers, deleting the "not so great" ones, editing the images, and then outputting them. There is no perfect workflow, and you will develop your own as you go. This chapter and the ones that follow will help you to create the workflow that is just right for you.

Chapter 1 Assignments

You might have already imported images using the Organizer, but here are a few things to practice just in case you haven't.

Make A Plan

Take a look at how your photos are currently stored on your computer. Are they kind of scattered around different folders depending on what you were doing or thinking at the time? Well, it's time to get organized. Spend a few minutes thinking about how best to organize your images. Write it down and make a tree diagram to help you plot your future imports.

Get Started with What You Already Have

Since you have just looked into your computer files to find your photos, why not go ahead and import them into the Organizer so that you can start your organization efforts right away. Remember that you can import anything from a single image right up to whole folders and subfolders. Start with something small before you just dump everything in, so that you can get the hang of things.

Time to Move from Camera to Computer

Even if you don't have a card full of images waiting to import, I'm sure you can find something to point your camera at to get a little practice. Or, if you are like some people I know, you have several months' worth of images just waiting for someplace to go. No time like the present. Hook up your camera or card reader and move them to their new home.

Life Moves Faster with Shortcuts

Earlier in the chapter I wrote about some keyboard shortcuts that can be used to make your repetitive tasks go a little faster. Try clicking the menus on the top bar and then look at the commands that come up. Functions that have keyboard shortcuts assigned to them will display the shortcut to the right of the function name. Try using a couple of them and then learn the ones that you will use the most. Over time, your work will go much faster and you will fly through your organizing and editing tasks.

Share your results with the book's Flickr group!

Join the group here: flickr.com/groups/elements_fromsnapshotstogreatshots

2

ISO 400
1/50 sec.
f/2.8
50mm lens

Keeping Track

HOW TO FIND THOSE PHOTOS
MONTHS DOWN THE ROAD

In Chapter 1, we covered the import process to successfully download your images, but that is just the first step. Your photographs will be of no use if you cannot find them when you need them. This is why it is so important to be organized right from the start. Luckily, the Elements Organizer has a lot of tools to help keep your images neat and tidy.

In this chapter, we are going to learn tasks like tagging, sorting, creating albums, and stacking images. All of these will help you organize your images so that, in the future, you will have a much easier time finding exactly the picture that you want to use. Not only that, but you will also have an easier method of getting rid of the photos that you don't want.

Let's jump into the Organizer and start sorting some images.

PORING OVER THE PICTURE

This image was captured late one afternoon on the San Francisco coast. I was out with some friends on a photo shoot, looking for some different vantage points from which to photograph the Golden Gate Bridge. We found this rocky slope with lots of little wildflowers, and I thought it might be a pretty good spot. My composition wasn't bad, but as you can see from the inset image, my exposure was off a bit, probably because of the bright glare coming in from the left side of the frame. I managed to save the shot with a little image processing in Camera Raw and the Elements Editor.

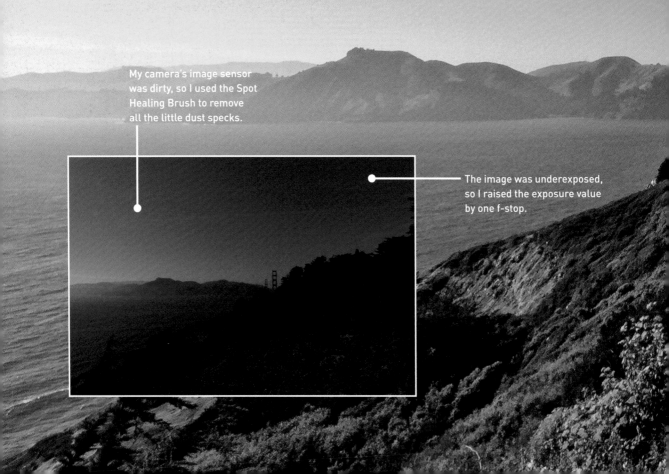

My camera's image sensor was dirty, so I used the Spot Healing Brush to remove all the little dust specks.

The image was underexposed, so I raised the exposure value by one f-stop.

I brightened up the shadow areas around the trees by using the Fill Light slider.

I changed the White Balance setting to Daylight, and I finished the image with a Clarity adjustment and sharpening.

ISO 200
1/200 sec.
f/22
18mm lens

TAGGING IMAGES WITH KEYWORDS

There are quite a few ways to find your photographs within the Organizer after you've imported them. One of my favorite ways to keep track of my images is to assign tags or keywords to them. Elements offers you several ways to do this, and it's one of the easiest methods for quickly locating images by subject matter. One of the great things about tagging your images is that you can apply multiple keywords so that your images will show up in a variety of categories. So let's say, for example, you like to take photographs of flowers. If you tag all of your flower photos with the keyword *flower*, you will then be able to see your entire collection of flower photos grouped together, even if they were shot and uploaded on different days. You can also assign multiple keywords so that you can be more specific in locating your images. For example, if you use the keywords *flower* and *red* every time you take a picture of a red flower, you can then locate all the similarly tagged images with just a few clicks of the mouse.

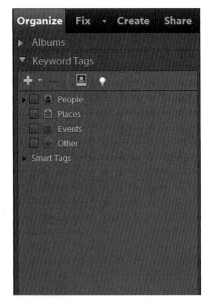

FIGURE 2.1
The Keyword Tags panel is in the Organize section.

Under the Organize tab of the Elements Organizer, you will see a section called Keyword Tags. Adobe has created several presets in this section that you can use right away, but the real power of the program is in creating custom keywords that relate directly to your images (**Figure 2.1**).

The easiest way to create a custom keyword tag is to click inside the text box at the bottom of the Keyword Tags panel (**Figure 2.2**) and type the keyword that you want to use for your images. In the Media Browser, select the photos that you want to assign that keyword to. Then, click the Apply button to create the new tag and assign it to the images. You will notice that your new tag has been added as a sub-tag of the Other tag field.

One of the nice features of the text box is that it will dynamically show you existing keywords as you begin to type. So if you've already used the keyword *Chinatown* and you have additional images you want to tag with it, type the letter *C* into the text box and you will see the word *Chinatown* appear in a list above the text box. Then all you have to do is click the word to fill in the rest (**Figure 2.3**).

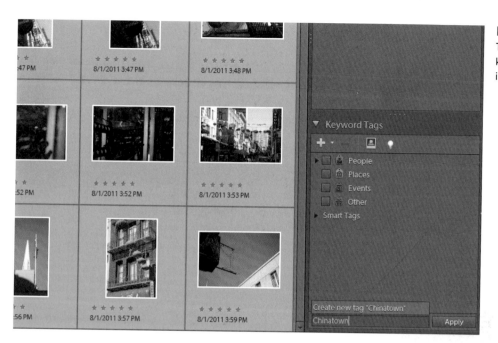

FIGURE 2.2
To add a custom keyword, just type it into the text box.

The real power of keyword tags is in the categories. Keywords can be sorted into broad categories and then narrowed down into sub-categories for greater sorting ability. For example, I like to travel a lot. To help keep track of my photos, I might want to have a parent category called Travel. Within that category, I could create a sub-category for each travel destination. This would make it much easier for me to locate the images that I want, rather than searching for the date that I actually traveled.

To create a new category, click the plus (+) icon under the Keyword Tags section and choose New Category. You can then choose the color of the tag, a category icon, and the name of the new category (**Figure 2.4**).

FIGURE 2.3
Typing in the text box will pull up a list of existing keywords.

CREATING A CATEGORY

1. Click the plus (+) icon, and then select New Category from the drop-down menu.

2. Click Choose Color, and select a tag color from the color picker (**A**).

3. Enter the new category name. In this instance, I type the word *Travel* (**B**).

4. Finally, select a category icon (**C**) for the new tag, and click the OK button.

FIGURE 2.4
You can customize new keyword categories with the Create Category options.

The category you created will now appear in the Keyword Tags list. If I want to create sub-categories within this parent category (for instance, *vacation* or *cruises*), I follow the same procedure for creating the category, but I select New Sub-Category. I type the name of the new sub-category, select the parent category, and click the OK button to finish. Depending on the level of organization that you want to achieve, you can create sub-categories within sub-categories. My preference is to create categories and then keywords that live within them. Your job is to find what works for you.

To create a keyword within a category, click the plus (+) icon and then select New Keyword Tag. The keyboard shortcut for doing this is Control-N (Command-N on a Mac). So why use the new keyword tag process if you can just type a new one like we did in the first example? The real benefit is that you get a lot more control over the information associated with that keyword tag.

By using the "create keyword tag" option, you can create a custom icon tag, assign the keyword to a category, name the keyword tag, and attach notes for more detailed information about the keyword. On my last trip to San Francisco, I took photographs in several different locations. Let's create some sub-categories and keyword tags to help me better organize those photographs.

CREATING SUB-CATEGORIES AND KEYWORDS

1. I want to create a new sub-category for the state that I visited, so I click the plus (+) icon and select New Sub-Category.

2. I type *California* in the Sub-Category Name field and then select Travel as the parent category (**Figure 2.5**).

3. I create a new sub-category, called San Francisco, that uses the new California tag as the parent (**Figure 2.6**).

4. Next, I use the keyboard shortcut Control-N (Command-N) to bring up the New Keyword dialog.

5. I type the new keyword *Chinatown* in the Name field (**Figure 2.7**).

6. I click the OK button to finish creating the keyword tag.

7. In the Media Browser, I select all of the images that I want to tag with this new keyword.

8. Finally, I drag and drop the Chinatown tag onto my selected images so that it will be applied to all of them.

FIGURE 2.5
Creating a sub-category.

FIGURE 2.6
It's possible to have sub-categories within sub-categories.

FIGURE 2.7
Adding a new keyword to a category.

FIGURE 2.8
After creating a custom keyword, you will see its tag in the keyword panel.

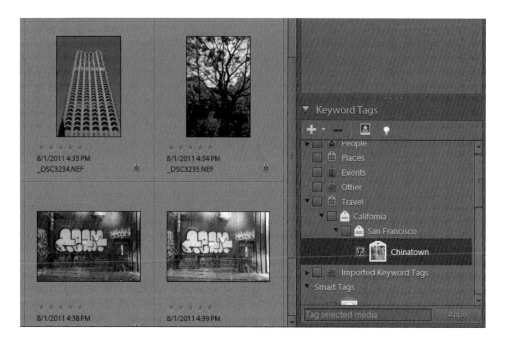

When this process is complete you will see two things. First, you will see a new thumbnail icon appear in the keyword tag (**Figure 2.8**). To edit this thumbnail icon, right-click the keyword tag, select Edit Keyword Tag, click the Edit Icon button, and select the image of your choice from the tagged files in the Media Browser (**Figure 2.9**). Second, you should see a small icon in the lower-right corner of the large thumbnails in the Media Browser, which indicates that the images have been tagged.

USING SMART TAGS

Using keyword tags is a highly effective way to keep track of your photographs, but it can be a little time consuming. The Organizer has the ability to apply Smart Tags, which will help you quickly organize your images without having to get into specific keyword tags. If you look in the Keyword Tags section of the Organizer, you will see the Smart Tags label at the bottom of the list (**Figure 2.10**). Click the disclosure triangle to see a list of Smart Tags that can be applied to your images. To apply a Smart Tag,

FIGURE 2.9
Selecting a thumbnail image for the new keyword tag.

you have to let the Organizer analyze your images first. To do this, select the images you want analyzed in the Media Browser, right-click, and choose Run Auto-Analyzer from the pop-up menu. Depending on the number of images that you have selected, this process can take a little while.

A progress bar will appear, letting you know where the Organizer is in the analyzing process. When the process is complete, you will see a small tag icon in the lower-right corner of each selected thumbnail. Go to the Smart Tags list in the Keyword Tags section and click the check boxes located to the left of each Smart Tag to see the images that received that tag in the Media Browser window. If no images received a particular tag, then the Media Browser window will be empty.

So how do you find out what tags were assigned to each image? The easy way is to position the mouse pointer over the top of the tag icon for one of the tagged images. As you hover over the tag icon, a label will appear, telling you which Smart Tags are assigned to that particular image. If you want to remove any of the tags that were applied during the Auto-Analyzer process, right-click the tag icon for the thumbnail and then select whichever tag you want removed.

FIGURE 2.10
Elements has several Smart Tags that can be automatically applied to your photos.

SELECTING IMAGES IN THE MEDIA BROWSER

There are a few ways to select images in the Media Browser. To select one image, click its thumbnail. To select multiple images that are not contiguous, click the first thumbnail and then hold the Control key (Command key on a Mac) while clicking additional photographs. To select a consecutive group of images, click the first image, scroll down to the last image you want to select, hold the Shift key, and click the last image; this will select everything from the first image down to the last image selected. If you want to select all of your images, use the keyboard shortcut Control-A (Command-A). To deselect, press Shift-Control-A (Shift-Command-A). All of these commands can also be found under the Edit menu.

SORTING IMAGES

It makes no sense to tag photographs if they aren't worth keeping. For that reason, we should probably discuss how to sort your images into two categories: those that you want to keep, and those that need to go in the trash. Performing this sorting process is good for a couple of reasons. First, it lets you focus on just those photographs that are keepers, while ignoring the poorer ones. Second, by identifying those photographs that you don't want to keep, you can delete them and recover some hard drive space.

The easiest way to sort through your images is to use the star rating system. You need to come up with your own system for rating your photographs, but the way I do it is to assign one star for those images that I want to delete and five stars for my definite keepers. Of course, you can choose to assign two, three, or four stars.

The first thing I do after importing new images is navigate to the first image and change the viewing mode of the Media Browser to Single Photo view. You do this by clicking the Single Photo View icon or dragging the thumbnail scaling slider all the way to the right. Now that I have made a larger view of my image, I press either the 1 key or the 5 key on the keyboard to assign one or five stars to the image. I can then use the left or right arrow keys to quickly view my images and assign a star rating to them. After I've assigned a star rating to all of the imported photographs, I switch back to a thumbnail view for the next step in the sorting process (**Figure 2.11**).

FIGURE 2.11
Thumbnails displaying their star ratings.

Now I can filter by the number of stars assigned to the image. I do this by clicking the star filter in the upper-right corner of the Media Browser. To find all of the images I want to delete, I click one star in the filter and then choose Only from the drop-down menu. Now I have a thumbnail view of all of the images I want to delete (**Figure 2.12**). To get rid of them, I click and drag across the images to select them, or click the first one and then click the last one while holding down the Shift key. The final step is to press the Delete key to remove the images from the Media Browser. Since we've already established that these are not keepers, it makes no sense to remove them from the Media Browser without also removing them from the hard drive, so I also select the "Also delete selected item(s) from the hard disk" check box (**Figure 2.13**). I click OK to delete the images from the catalog as well as from the hard drive.

FIGURE 2.12
Clicking one star in the filter will hide all photos with a different rating.

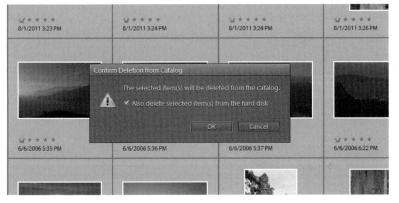

FIGURE 2.13
Select the check box to delete the images from the hard drive.

FIGURE 2.14
The Create Album Category options.

FIGURE 2.15
You can add images to an album by dragging them into the Content area of the album.

After I've eliminated all of my bad images, I go back to the filter and click the five-stars filter. Now that I no longer need to sort my images, I can remove the star ratings by selecting all of the images and pressing the 0 (zero) key. Of course, you may choose to use the stars for your own rating system. It's completely up to you.

CREATING ALBUMS

Albums are a way of grouping your images into meaningful collections. You can create albums for just about any purpose. They're not tied to any specific folder on your hard drive or any group of photographs, but they are a way for you to group meaningful images into one collection. And just like with keyword tags, you can use parent albums and sub-albums to further organize your files. Let's say you want to create an album called Birthdays. You might then create sub-albums for Johnny and Mary and whoever else you have birthday photos of. Or maybe you want to create a parent album called Vacations. Then every time you take a vacation, you can create a sub-album specifically for those photos and put them in the Vacations album. You might also want to create parent albums for specific purposes. Let's say you're collecting images that you want to put up on a Web site. You could create an album called For the Web and then add the desired images from your catalog.

I like to lead and participate in photowalks. In order to help me locate and organize my photowalk images, I'm going to create a couple of albums. The first order of business is creating the parent album category. Here's how the process would go.

CREATING AN ALBUM AND AN ALBUM CATEGORY

1. In the Albums section of the Organize tab, click the plus (+) button and select New Album Category (**Figure 2.14**).
2. Type the name of the album category in the text box, and select a parent album category if desired. Click the OK button.
3. Click the plus (+) button once again, and select New Album.
4. Select a category from the Album Category drop-down list.
5. Type the album name into the text box.
6. Drag images from the Media Browser and drop them into the content window (**Figure 2.15**).
7. Click the Done button when you're finished adding images.

There should now be a new album with the name you selected in the Album panel, and each associated image will have an album icon in the lower-right corner. If you want to see what album an image is associated with, hover the mouse pointer over the icon and an info box will pop up with the album name. It is possible to have the same image appear in multiple albums. If this is the case, each album name will display in the pop-up text.

If you want to add additional images to a particular album, all you have to do is drag them into the desired album in the Albums section of the Organize tab. You can also drag the album onto any thumbnail in the Media Browser to add that image to the album. To view all of the images in an album, click the album name and you will see only those images associated with that album in the Media Browser window. To remove an image from an album, right-click the image and then select Remove from Album from the pop-up menu.

SORTING WITH SMART ALBUMS

There may be times when you want to sort your photographs by certain criteria, such as file type, file name, or the information found in the photograph's metadata. The Smart Album is the tool that will let you apply these search criteria to your images in order to group them into one album. So why use this particular feature? Here's an example of why I would use it.

I write a lot of books about cameras. In those books, I need specific examples of photographs taken under certain conditions. For example, if I need images that were taken with a high ISO setting, I can use a Smart Album to quickly locate photographs that meet that criterion.

CREATING A SMART ALBUM

1. Click the plus (+) icon, and select New Smart Album (**Figure 2.16**).

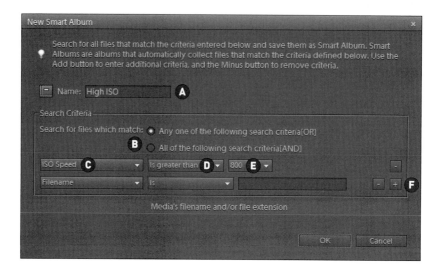

2. Give your new Smart Album a name by typing it in the Name text box (**A**).

3. Now it's time to figure out what the search criteria will be. Select the option to search for files that match "Any of the following search criteria" or the option to search for files that match "All of the following search criteria" (**B**).

4. Click the first drop-down, and select the criterion you want to include in your album search (I'm looking for ISO Speed) (**C**).

5. In the next box, select the variable for that criterion (such as *is* or *starts with* or, in my case, *is greater than*) (**D**).

6. The final variable depends on the item being searched. You may have to fill in the blank or choose from a list of options (**E**).

7. It's possible to have more than one search criterion for the album. To add more criteria, click the Add (+) button on the right side of the Search Criteria section to add an additional line (**F**).

8. After you have defined your search criteria, click the OK button to create the new Smart Album.

If you want to remove any of the search criteria, click the Minus (–) button to the right of the criteria fields. Smart Albums have blue album icons; regular albums have light-green icons.

The great thing about Smart Albums is that they will constantly monitor your catalog for images that meet your search criteria. You may have noticed that there is a Smart Album already created for you called Last 6 Months, which monitors all of your photos and will let you display only those images that were taken in the last six months. This search is based on the actual capture date, not the date that the image was imported. If you recently imported images that were taken last year, don't use this album to find them.

You could, however, find all the pictures you took last year by creating a new Smart Album and then having it search for a specific date range. See how cool that is?

To modify the criteria used to create a Smart Album, click the Smart Album's name in the Albums list and then click the Options button at the top of the Media Browser window. This will bring up the Smart Album dialog, where you can tweak your search settings.

TIP

Unlike regular albums, Smart Albums don't apply any icon to the images. That's because they could change status depending on the search criteria used. They will, however, group the images into different batches in the Media Browser based on their import dates.

SEEING ALL OF YOUR IMAGES

Sorting images using keywords and albums is a great way of locating specific images in your catalog. By clicking either the album or the keyword, your Media Browser will display only those images associated with your selection. To quickly get back to viewing all of the images in your catalog, click the Show All button at the top of the Media Browser window.

STACKING IMAGES

Stacks are a great feature because they let you group photos and allow you to only see the top image in the stack while viewing your thumbnails. Let's say you have a bunch of similar pictures of the Golden Gate Bridge. You can simply select all of them and then combine them into one stack of images. You see just one of them in the Media Browser, but all the others are there, waiting for you to unstack them when you are ready. It's kind of like a deck of cards, where you only see the top card in the deck. The real advantage to doing this is that it cleans up the Media Browser so you have fewer thumbnails to look through.

CREATING A STACK

1. Start by selecting the images you want to stack. You can select as many images as you want, but you need at least two.

2. Choose Edit > Stack > Stack Selected Photos (or use the keyboard shortcut Control-Alt-S for Windows or Command-Option-S for Mac) (**Figure 2.17**).

FIGURE 2.17
The Stack command is in the Edit menu.

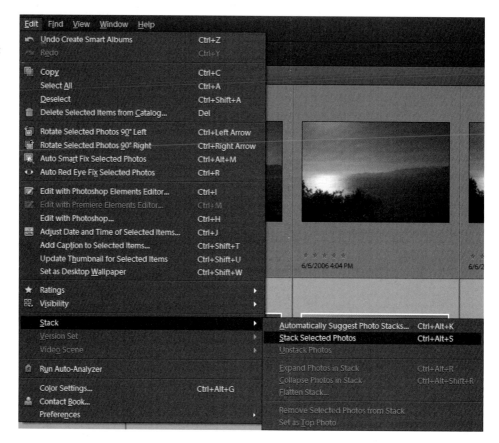

That's all there is to it—just two small steps to clean up the clutter. When you are done, you will see a stack icon in the upper-right corner of the thumbnail that represents the stack. There is also an arrow icon on the right side of the thumbnail frame (**Figure 2.18**); click it to unstack the images. The arrow will reverse direction when the images are unstacked and appear on the last image in the stack. Just click it to restack the images again.

FIGURE 2.18
The right-facing
arrows indicate
stacked images.

USING SUGGESTED PHOTO STACKS

If you are feeling adventurous, you can select a large group of images and then let
the Organizer give you stacking suggestions. I really love this feature because the
image search engine does a fantastic job of grouping duplicate images. Once it has
sorted them, it displays the suggested stacks in a search window, with each stack on
a new line. All that is required is to click either the Stack or Unstack button for each
group. Unique photos will appear in a grouping at the bottom of the window. You
can also drag images from one suggested stack into another. If, for some reason,
you end up with a couple of images that seem to be unrelated to the others in the
suggested group, you can simply drag them into the Unique Photos section. When
all of the stacking is done, click the Done button and you are returned to the Media
Browser, where all of your new stacks are waiting for you.

GETTING A BETTER VIEW

One of the reasons that the Organizer works so well is that it can be customized to your preferences. There are several different options available for displaying your images and image information, and each one of those can be customized to your lik-ing. Now, when I say customized, I don't mean that you can change all of the content to only display what you want, but that you can drag the dividers between the differ-ent panels to resize them into an arrangement that is perfect for you.

THUMBNAILS

The default view in the Media Browser is to show images in a thumbnail configu-ration. The default size of the thumbnails may be just to your liking, but if it isn't, you're in luck, because you can control just how large or small the thumbnails are. To change the size of the thumbnails, move the thumbnail slider at the top of the Media Browser (**Figure 2.19**). To make thumbnails incrementally larger, press Control- + (plus) (Command- +). To make thumbnails incrementally smaller, press Control- – (minus) (Command- –).

FIGURE 2.19
The thumbnail size can be changed using the slider and controls at the top of the Media Browser.

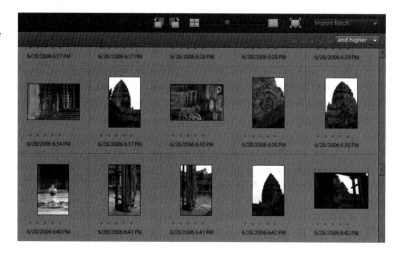

SINGLE PHOTO VIEW

If you really want a good look at your image, you can take it into Single Photo view. Do this by moving the thumbnail slider all the way to the right, clicking the Single Photo icon to the right of the slider, or double-clicking the image. While in Single Photo view, you can add a caption to your image by clicking the "Click here to add caption" text under the image (**Figure 2.20**). To return to the thumbnail view, double-click the image once more.

FIGURE 2.20
Single Photo view.

FULL SCREEN VIEW

What's that you say? You tried Single Photo view but it still wasn't enough for you and your 30-inch mega-screen? Well then, maybe it's time you moved into Full Screen view. Look for the button to the right of the thumbnail size slider (it's just to the right of the Single Photo icon). When you hover the mouse pointer over the icon, you will see a pop-up that says View, Edit, Organize in Full Screen – F11. That's your clue to click it and go large. Another option for going full screen is to click the Display Options icon in the upper-right portion of the screen and look for the View, Edit, Organize in Full Screen option in the drop-down menu. You may have also noticed that the keyboard shortcut to jump into Full Screen view is F11. If you are using a

Mac, make sure that the F11 key is not already assigned to another function, as is usually the case.

When you are in Full Screen view, there are a few things you can do to have a little fun. First, you can zoom in and out of the image using the same keyboard shortcuts I described for changing thumbnail sizes. If you have a mouse with a scroll wheel, you can use it to change the zoom view of your image. Click the image to zoom in to a 100 percent view. You can use the mouse to move the image around at this magnification. Click once again to zoom back out to a "fit screen" view.

To browse a slideshow of your images, press the spacebar or click the play button at the bottom of the screen (**Figure 2.21**). To stop, press the pause button. To manually move through the pictures, use the left arrow and right arrow keys on your keyboard; there is also a set of left and right arrows next to the play button that will do the same thing.

FIGURE 2.21
Maximize your image by using Full Screen view.

If you want to jump to a specific image, you can launch the Film Strip view. Click the button on the far left of the play button or use the keyboard shortcut Control-F (Command-F). This will bring up a thumbnail strip of images on the right side of your screen that you can quickly scroll through. Click an image in the strip to see the full-screen version.

To exit the Full Screen view, click the X on the right side of the control panel or press the Escape key.

USING FULL SCREEN VIEW AS A SLIDESHOW

The Full Screen view is a great way of giving a slideshow of your images, but here's a little suggestion. Create an album of the images that you want to use in the show first. Once the images are in the album, you can drag them into whatever order you like. Then click the first image in the album, launch Full Screen view, and click the play button to begin your customized show.

VIEWING IMAGE PROPERTIES

This little gem of an info box is turned off by default, but I always end up turning it on and docking it to the bottom of the right-hand panel. To access image info, select an image and then select Window > Properties. You can also use the keyboard shortcut Alt-Enter (Option-Enter).

The Properties panel contains four groups of information related to your image. The first is General, which you can see by clicking the left-most icon (it looks like a piece of paper in front of a blue box). General is where you will see the image file name, any captions or notes you added to the file, ratings, size, time of capture, and file location. You can also use this area to add notes or captions by typing in the appropriate text box (**Figure 2.22**).

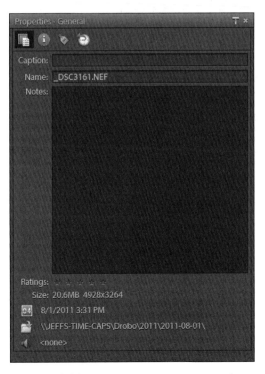

FIGURE 2.22
The General section of the Properties panel.

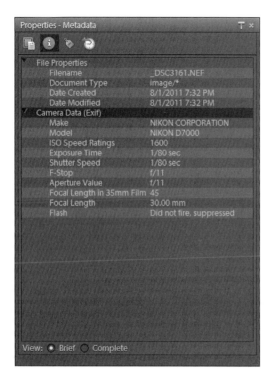

The Metadata section displays the camera shooting data for the image.

FIGURE 2.23
The Metadata section displays the camera shooting data for the image.

Click the info button (the blue dot with the letter *i* in the middle) for access to all of the image metadata. Metadata is the information recorded to the image by your camera, and it includes such things as date, time, camera model, lens, shutter speed, ISO, and so on. To see a more extensive list of metadata, click the Complete radio button at the bottom of the panel (**Figure 2.23**).

The other two Properties views will allow you to see any keyword tags associated with the image, and the image's history.

To dock the Properties panel to your task pane, click the small T-shaped icon on the right side of the Image Properties title bar. This will add the panel underneath the keyword tags. To undock, simply click that same icon (it changes shape just a little when docked), or click the small X on the title bar to close the panel completely.

Chapter 2 Assignments

Now that you have imported some images, let's get organized. Here are a few assignments to get you going.

Get Familiar with the Organizer

Your sorting and tagging will go better if you are comfortable with how your workspace is organized. Adjust your thumbnails so that you can see them comfortably. Then go into Single Photo view and use the left arrow and right arrow keys to skim through your images. Put the mouse pointer between the panels and try resizing them as well. Want to get rid of that task pane for a while? Look in the Window menu for the Hide Task Pane command. Press F11 to go full screen and get familiar with all that real estate.

Tags Are Key

Look at some of your images in the Media Browser and see if they have some qualities in common. Now create a keyword and try tagging them. Remember that you can use multiple keywords on one image. After you have a few different keywords, try isolating those images in the Media Browser by selecting the check boxes next to the keywords in the Keyword Tag panel.

Time for Some Albums

Remember that keywords and albums are different and yet very similar. Create an album called Email and then move some photos in there that you can send off to family and friends. (If you aren't sure how to do that quite yet, don't worry. We will cover that in a later chapter.)

Clean Up Thumbnails with Stacks

Try selecting all of the photos from one of your shoots or import sessions. Now let the Organizer suggest some image stacks. When you are happy with the stacks, click Done, locate all of your individual stacks, and try unstacking them to get a feel for it.

Share your results with the book's Flickr group!

Join the group here: flickr.com/groups/elements_fromsnapshotstogreatshots

3

ISO 200
1/15 sec.
f/5.6
40mm lens

Basic Fixes

USING THE AUTOMATED TOOLS

Now that your images are imported and sorted, it's time to go over some ways to make them look better. As we move further into the book, we will cover advanced image editing, where your control over the process and results is the ultimate goal. But there will be times when you just want a quick fix. Maybe the image looks pretty darn good right out of the camera and just needs a little tweak. Well, there are some tools that you can access right from the Organizer to fix common problems and let you quickly get on to fun stuff like emailing or sharing your images. Just remember that Auto usually means you don't have much control, so you basically take what you get.

If you are looking for more control and maybe a little help along the way, you can turn to the Quick or Guided edits. These procedures will let you select more options and make some decisions. They are built with limited control, but they will allow you more flexibility in your edits. Whether you want the software to fix it or you'd like a little more control, there is a place for Auto, Quick, and Guided edits in your workflow.

PORING OVER THE PICTURE

The original raw image was processed in Camera Raw, where I applied the Vivid camera calibration so the colors would really pop.

I warmed up the white balance a little to compensate for the smoky blue light in the room.

The background was converted to black and white using the Convert to Black and White feature in the Enhance menu.

ISO 500
1/40 sec.
f/4
85mm lens

The lanterns were selected using the Quick Selection tool and then cleaned up a little with the Refine Edge option. The selected lanterns were then placed on their own layer.

There is something magical about Chinese paper lanterns. I'm not sure what it is that makes them so appealing. Perhaps it's the bright colors and golden tassels. Maybe it's because you never see just one and there are many compositional possibilities. I know that it's hard for me to pass them by without taking at least a few photos. This shot was taken in a temple in Malaysia. You can see from the original inset image that the background was light and smoky because of the incense burning all around. Instead of trying to improve the background, I decided to make it black and white and let the lanterns take center stage.

AUTO EDITS

First, let me say that I am not necessarily an advocate for automatic image processing. Much as with the Auto modes on a camera, you have to give up control and decision-making to a computer program that uses algorithms to determine what is best for your photograph. Sometimes it gets it right, and sometimes not so much.

The point here is that there are times when you just want something quick and easy to correct a small problem and don't want to labor with the full Editor, especially for something like a quick contrast or color adjustment. In those instances, a quick Auto fix might just be what you need.

AUTO SMART FIX

The automatic options can be found right within the Organizer. Click the Fix tab and you will find a list of quick adjustment tools at your disposal. At the top of the list is the Auto Smart Fix tool. It's kind of like the jack-of-all-trades in that it doesn't just adjust one issue within your image. Instead, it looks at the entire photo and makes corrections to color, sharpness, brightness, contrast, the works. It is the autopilot of image correction, and about the only thing it won't do for you is cropping.

FIGURE 3.1
Edited images will be stacked with the originals.

When you click the Auto Smart Fix tool, Elements creates a new duplicate image to edit so that it doesn't damage your original. Typically, it creates the same type of image, so if you are editing a JPEG, it will create a duplicate JPEG with the word *edited* appended to the file name so you know which is which (**Figure 3.1**). It automatically stacks this new, edited version with the original. The edited version will be the visible image on top of the stack.

If you use any of the Auto fixes on a raw image file, you will be presented with a dialog informing you that Elements cannot write to a raw file. It will ask you to select a new file type, such as JPEG or TIFF, for the edited version of your file (**Figure 3.2**).

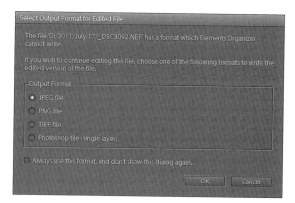

FIGURE 3.2
Raw file types require you to select a new file format for your edited versions.

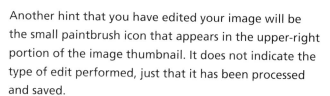

FIGURE 3.3
The Auto Smart Fix button is in the Fix panel of the Organizer.

Another hint that you have edited your image will be the small paintbrush icon that appears in the upper-right portion of the image thumbnail. It does not indicate the type of edit performed, just that it has been processed and saved.

To apply the Auto Smart Fix tool to your image, select the image that you wish to apply it to in the Organizer, click the Fix tab, and then click the Auto Smart Fix option (**Figure 3.3**). It's automated from there, and you will soon see a new and hopefully improved version of your image show up in the Organizer.

You can also access the Auto Smart Fix option by right-clicking any image in the Organizer and then selecting Auto Smart Fix from the pop-up menu (**Figure 3.4**).

If Auto Smart Fix is the jack-of-all-trades, then the rest of the Auto edits are the specialists. Each one addresses a specific area of processing. They can also be used in combination with the other Auto edits, including Auto Smart Fix.

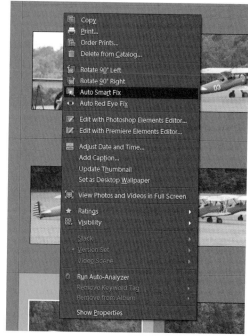

FIGURE 3.4
You can quickly access the Auto Smart Fix option by right-clicking a thumbnail.

AUTO COLOR

Depending on how your picture was taken, the colors you see in the photograph may be pretty accurate, but they could also be suffering from a little bit of a color cast. You can often find an example of a color cast in a photograph that was taken in the shade. Even when it is sunny outside, blue skies can give everything a slightly blue look, and this is especially true when photographing a subject in the shade. The Auto Color option will attempt to adjust for the color cast and improve the contrast. It is usually a subtle fix that may not be very visible in your image (**Figure 3.5**).

AUTO LEVELS

Within every image is a range of tones that usually goes from light to dark. The Auto Levels adjustment will try to equalize the tones in your picture so that you have a better range of tones. This means the blacks won't be so dark and the whites won't be so light. I find that I usually have more success by using the Auto Contrast tool.

AUTO CONTRAST

Sometimes when you make contrast adjustments, the colors can be influenced in a bad way. Increasing the contrast will result in higher color saturations. Decreasing the contrast in an image can have the opposite effect, where colors might look less vibrant. The Auto Contrast tool tries to improve the overall contrast in the image without affecting the colors.

Whether you use the Auto Levels or Auto Contrast option is up to you, but Auto Contrast would be my choice for an image that is flat or lacking good contrast (**Figure 3.6**). Both options will render a similar result, so the best thing to do is to try each one and then delete the one with the less desirable result (**Figure 3.7**).

FIGURE 3.6
The original image
is flat and lacking in
contrast.

FIGURE 3.7
The photo on the
left had an Auto
Levels adjust-
ment applied;
the photo on the
right received the
Auto Contrast
adjustment.

AUTO SHARPEN

Most images need a little sharpening. If you are shooting in the standard JPEG format, a little bit of sharpness will be added to your image as it is being saved, but it
may not be adequate for your subject. It's not possible to know just how much sharpening will be added during the Auto Sharpen operation, so you will just need to give
it a click and see if it meets your needs.

The best way to see the results of Auto Sharpen is to view your image at 100%.
After applying Auto Sharpen, click the Full Screen icon or press the F11 key to go
to Full Screen view, and then click the image once to zoom to 100%.

FIGURE 3.8
After you apply Auto Red Eye Fix, a dialog will pop up to alert you that the image is being stacked. Select the check box if you don't want to see this dialog again.

AUTO RED EYE FIX

Most cameras today do a fantastic job of eliminating red eye in your subjects. With the use of pre-flashes or red-eye reduction lamps, it is rare that any of those demon-eyed subjects ever show their faces in the Organizer. Every now and then, though, the circumstances are just right (or wrong) for a little red eye, and then you get the chance to try out the Auto Red Eye Fix tool.

Just as with the other Auto fixes, all you need to do is select the image in the Organizer and then click the Auto Red Eye Fix option. Everything from that point is taken care of for you. If the tool locates red eyes in the image, an info window will pop up telling you that the operation was performed successfully and that the image is now stacked with the original (**Figure 3.8**). The resulting image is usually pretty amazing, but keep in mind that your results will vary depending on the severity of the red eye in the image (**Figure 3.9**).

FIGURE 3.9
The Auto Red Eye Fix tool does an amazing job, as you can see from these images.

CROP

All of the fixes we have looked at so far have been automatic, requiring nothing more than the click of a button. The Crop tool in the Fix panel is not really an automatic tool, but this version is a little limited in functionality and does not require using the Elements Editor, so I thought it might fit into this section.

With an image selected, click the Crop tool in the Fix panel. The image will open in a new dialog window (**Figure 3.10**). Click the Crop tool and then drag your cursor across the image. A crop window will appear and let you determine what to leave in and what to get rid of in your picture. You can use the original image size ratio, create a custom size, or select one of the pre-sized ratios (square, 4x6, 3x4, 5x7, and 8x10) from the Aspect Ratio drop-down menu. Resize by clicking one of the corners of the crop guide and dragging it. If you place the mouse cursor in the middle of the crop guide, you can then drag the crop selection all around the image. Click the OK button to complete the crop.

FIGURE 3.10
The Crop Photo dialog.

The one thing I don't like about this Crop tool is that there is no way to rotate the crop guide. This is very important for images that are a little cockeyed and need straightening. If, however, your image is straight and just needs some quick cropping, then this is the tool for you.

ADDING CONTROL WITH QUICK EDITS IN THE EDITOR

There's only so much that can be done in the Organizer, so if you want more control and more options you will need to move into the Elements Editor. Launch the Editor by clicking the Fix tab in the Organizer and then clicking the Edit Photos option. You can also use the keyboard shortcut Control-I for Windows or Command-I on a Mac. It will help if you have an image selected before moving into the Editor. To start without going to the Organizer, click the Start button in Windows and select Adobe Photoshop Elements from the Programs area (for Mac users, look for Adobe Photoshop Elements in your Applications folder). A splash screen will open, allowing you to select either the Organizer or the Editor (**Figure 3.11**).

My advice is that you work from the Organizer and then go to the Editor as needed. The two programs were made to work hand in hand, and it will be easier for you to go back and find new images to work with if you already have the Organizer open.

FIGURE 3.11
You can jump right into the Editor from the splash screen when you start Elements.

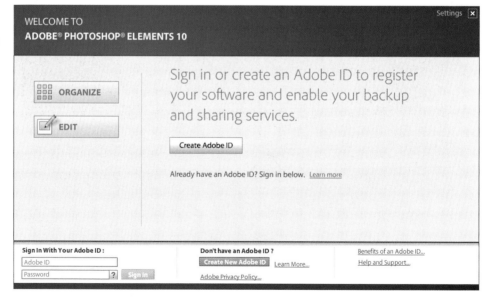

WORKING WITH MULTIPLE IMAGES

To make your workflow more efficient, try taking multiple files with you from the Organizer into the Editor. First, select the images in the Organizer. Then enter the Editor as you would with just a single image. Now look at the bottom of the editing workspace. You should see thumbnails of the images you selected in the Project Bin. Double-click images in the Project Bin to quickly pull them into the active workspace (**Figure 3.12**).

FIGURE 3.12
The Project Bin at the bottom of the screen shows you all of the files that are currently opened in the Editor.

FIGURE 3.13
The Quick fixes can be found under the Edit tab.

To access the Quick edits, click the Edit panel on the right side of the screen and then choose the Quick tab (**Figure 3.13**). Quick edits offer some of the same editing solutions as the Auto tools in the Organizer but with more control over how much of the fix is applied. Those of you who love sliders may find yourself addicted to the Quick edits.

SMART FIX

This slider uses the same algorithms as the Auto Smart Fix feature, but with one very important difference: You can choose how much of the effect is applied to the image. To start fixing your image, drag the slider to the right. Hey, it's not called a Quick edit for nothing. When the image looks good, just stop sliding. I prefer to move it all the way to the right and then back it off until it looks just right.

If you want a visual representation of how things will look, click the disclosure triangle to the right of the slider. This will open a 9 by 9 grid of thumbnails with varying amounts of the fix applied. As you move the cursor over each thumbnail, the image in the main display changes to reflect your selection. You will also see the slider jumping from position to position as you move from preview to preview. If you like one preview but want to make a fine adjustment, drag left or right to make subtle changes. You can reset everything by clicking the top-left preview or sliding the slider all the way back to the left.

TIP

All of the Quick edit adjustments work the same way, with sliders as well as previews to help make your edits. You can also use the sliders together, making adjustments in all of them or just one or two. It's all up to you.

A big difference between the Auto fixes and the Quick fixes is the amount of fix applied. The Auto fixes make "best guess" changes. The Quick fix sliders allow you to go beyond the usually minimal changes and make large adjustments. If, however, you want to see what the effect would be by using the Auto setting, you don't need to go back to the Organizer. There is an Auto option for the Smart Fix, Levels, Contrast, Color, and Sharpness sliders that will apply the same results as found in the Auto fixes. If the Auto fix isn't enough, apply more by using the sliders.

LIGHTING

This fix is a combination of two of the Auto adjustments we covered (Levels and Contrast) with an additional three sliders that are some of my favorites here in the Quick panel. In the Lighting section, you will see that the Levels and Contrast adjustments only have an Auto option. The real fun here is playing with the Shadows, Midtones, and Highlights sliders, which can do some amazing things for your images.

The Shadows slider will brighten dark shadows in your image, allowing you to see more details in the dark areas. The Midtones slider is set with the slide control in the middle, not on the left side of the bar. That's because you can apply positive (to the right) and negative (to the left) adjustments. Moving this slider will either increase or decrease contrast in the image. The Highlights slider will help with things like bright skies and clouds by letting you darken just the brightest parts of the image. That's what is so special about these sliders—they adjust certain aspects of the image without affecting the rest. It allows you to really focus on the problem areas (**Figure 3.14**).

COLOR AND BALANCE

If you aren't happy with the colors in your image, you can give them a little boost or dull them down a bit using the Saturation slider. The Hue slider will actually change the colors in the image. The best way to experience it is to just slide it back and forth. Truthfully, I don't think you will use the Hue slider much, but the Saturation slider can definitely liven up your photos. Just be careful not to go too overboard with this one.

FIGURE 3.14
The Shadows slider in the Lighting section allowed the letters in the sign to be brightened without affecting the sky.

If, for some reason, you had the wrong white balance set on your camera, the Balance slider can help you correct the problem. The Tint slider can make adjustments to images that are either too green or too magenta. Usually these tint adjustments are needed when you shoot in artificial light.

SHARPNESS

I much prefer the Quick Sharpen tool to the Auto Sharpen tool, although that option is available here as well. The key to sharpening is to do it with your image at 100% view. Then you will see an accurate portrayal of how the sharpening is affecting your image. The easiest way to enlarge your view to 100% is to use the keyboard shortcut Control-1 (Command-1). Then select the Hand tool by pressing the H key or clicking the tool in the Editor toolbar (**Figure 3.15**). With the Hand tool selected, move your image around in the viewing window so that you are looking at an area that is in focus and that should be very sharp. Then move the Sharpen slider until you are satisfied with the amount of sharpening. When you are done, press Control-0 (Command-0) or click the Fit Screen button above the toolbar to see your entire image again.

FIGURE 3.15
The Hand tool, along with the other Quick edit tools, is located in the toolbar on the left side of the editing screen.

CROP

There isn't a Crop slider in the Quick panel, but if you look in the toolbar you will find the Crop tool nestled between the Red Eye and Quick Selection tools. This tool works similarly to the Crop tool in the Organizer except it doesn't need to open in its own window. After clicking the tool or simply tapping the C key, choose the Aspect Ratio setting. Leaving it set to No Restrictions means that you can freeform crop your image without regard to length versus width. If you want your crop to have the same aspect ratio as the original image, select Use Photo Ratio from the drop-down list. After you've set the aspect ratio, drag on your image to choose a new crop.

The benefit of cropping in Quick mode as opposed to using the Crop tool in the Organizer is that it allows you to rotate the crop selection. This means that you can eliminate unwanted areas from your image and straighten it at the same time. To rotate the crop guide, move your cursor to one of the corners on the outside area of the crop guide. You should see a double-ended arrow that looks bent in the middle. Click it and pull up or down; you'll see your crop guide start to rotate. To resize the guide, put the cursor right on the corner and the arrows will turn from bent to straight. Then, just drag toward or away from the center of the image (**Figure 3.16**).

What if you want to change the crop orientation altogether? No problem. To the right of the Aspect Ratio drop-down list, you will see the width and height of the crop. Between the two settings are two arrows facing opposite directions. Give them a click, and it will switch your numbers. Now you can, for example, draw a vertical crop guide inside a horizontal image (**Figure 3.17**).

FIGURE 3.16
Rotate your crop and straighten an image by dragging the corners.

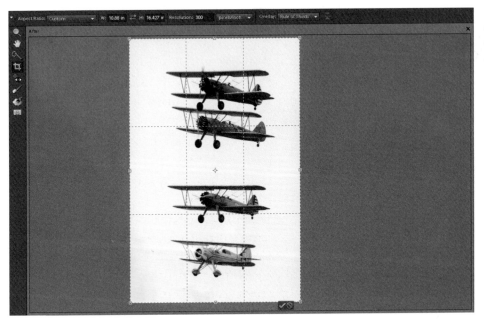

FIGURE 3.17
Change your crop orientation to create a whole new look for your image.

SELECTIVE EDITS

You may have noticed some other tools in the toolbar besides the Hand and Crop tools. The Zoom tool is shaped like a magnifying glass and is self-explanatory. The Quick Selection tool requires a little explanation, but once you use it, you will find it indispensable.

QUICK SELECTION

Simply put, the Quick Selection tool allows you to select portions of your image by painting with the tool as if it were a brush. After you have made a selection, you can do things to the selected area without affecting the rest of the image. To demonstrate, I have a photo of a biplane, and I would like to lighten the bottom of the wing. If I use only the Lighting tools, I will have to lighten the entire image. Instead, I will paint a selection on the wing using the Quick Selection tool.

The tool can be used to add to or subtract from a selection. Start with a simple click of the tool in an area you want to select. If it selects too small an area, increase the size of the brush by pressing the right bracket key (]). Pressing the left bracket key ([) makes the brush smaller and more precise. Click different areas to add to your selection. If any portion is added to the selection that doesn't belong, hold down the Alt key (Option key on a Mac) while clicking to subtract from the selection. In **Figure 3.18**, you will see that I have used the tool to select the underside of the wing, which is represented by the dotted lines. I can now use the Lighting tools to make corrections to only the selected area. When the edit to the selection is done, choose Select > Deselect or press Control-D (Command-D) (**Figure 3.19**).

> **TIP**
>
> Those dotted lines you see around a selection are often referred to in photo editing as "marching ants." Make a selection and you'll soon understand why.

FIGURE 3.18
The underside
of the wing was
isolated from the
rest of the photo
by using the Quick
Selection tool.

FIGURE 3.19
The Quick Selection
tool allowed the
shadows under the
wing to be bright-
ened independently
of the rest of the
image.

RED EYE REMOVAL

This might be one of the easiest tools in the whole bunch. Zoom in on the red eye and drag a selection over the eye. When you let go of the mouse button, the red eye is automatically fixed. The difference between this and the Auto version is that there are a couple of options that you can set for the tool. The options, like those for most tools in the toolbar, are located just above the toolbar. You can enlarge or reduce the pupil size and also determine how much to darken it. I wouldn't go changing anything until you try the default settings of 50 and 50. They work for the majority of cases.

To quickly fix a red eye problem, select the tool and then drag out a box over the eye (**Figure 3.20**). The fix happens as soon as you finish drawing the box. It doesn't get much easier than that.

FIGURE 3.20

Quickly remove red eyes by dragging a box with the Red Eye Removal tool.

WHITEN TEETH

Sometimes you don't need a lot of explanation for a tool, and this would be one of those times. In these days of cola and coffee, sometimes your subject's teeth aren't looking their best. If that's the case, just grab this tool and paint over their teeth for instant whitening. It automatically selects the teeth while you are painting over them, and when done, instant white! I leave it to you as to whether or not to send them the dentist bill.

MAKE DULL SKIES BLUE

We will cover some other methods for creating better-looking skies, but for a quick fix, it's hard to beat the Make Dull Skies Blue brush (yes, that's really what it's called). It uses smart selection technology to allow you to quickly paint over your dull skies. As you do, it starts filling in a more vibrant looking sky (**Figure 3.21**). The only problem I have with it is that it is often too blue for my tastes. If you also think that is the case, here's what you do.

After completing your selection and coloring the sky, press Control-D (Command-D) to get rid of the selection. Now switch the Editor into Full mode by clicking the Full tab in the Edit panel (it's located in the upper-right portion of the screen). Look in the middle of the panel for the Layers section, and you will see a layer with a small black and white thumbnail of your selection (**Figure 3.22**). Click the Opacity menu and lower the opacity to something more to your liking, say 50% (**Figure 3.23**). We will do more work in the Layers panel in later chapters.

FIGURE 3.22
The Make Dull Skies Blue tool creates a layer that can be adjusted to reduce the blue sky effect.

FIGURE 3.23
The skies in the original image (top) are flat and boring, but the Make Dull Skies Blue brush added more saturated color as well as a bit of a gradient to the final image (bottom).

BLACK AND WHITE

The last selective edit tool, called Black and White – High Contrast, allows you to selectively turn portions of your image into black and white. It uses smart selection technology, so it will instantly look for edges while you paint with it. This is not necessarily the tool that you should use to create a totally black and white image, but if you want to isolate a subject and make it stand out, you can do some really great things with it. My preference is to have a main subject in color and then paint the background in black and white (**Figure 3.24**).

FIGURE 3.24
The lanterns were isolated and really stand out thanks to the Black and White brush.

GUIDED EDITS

The Guided edits live in the Edit panel and are there to help you through some of the operations we have just covered (**Figure 3.25**). I like to think of this panel as having two parts. The three sections in the first part allow you to perform routine image editing and enhancements. There are guides that will show you how to crop, lighten and darken, adjust contrast, and fix color and lighting. The sections in the second part lean toward special effects, like creating a Lomo effect, creating a picture stack (**Figure 3.26**), replacing faces in a group shot, and general whiz-bang stuff like that. They can be a lot of fun, but we are not going to cover them because they are guided and don't require a lot of explanation. They are something you will want to play with when you have mastered fixing your photos.

FIGURE 3.25
Guided edits will
walk you step by
step through some
basic edits and
special effects.

FIGURE 3.26
This image was
created using the
Picture Stack option
in the Guided edits.

Chapter 3 Assignments

It can be very satisfying to work on an image and transform it from a simple snapshot into something that might be worthy of hanging on your walls. But that's certainly not the goal with every image we take. Sometimes you just need to give a photo a little tweak before emailing it to a friend or posting it to a social networking site. Or perhaps there is something in the photo that should be cropped out. The reasons for needing a quick fix are numerous, and hopefully this chapter has shown you some easy ways to make them happen. Let's try a few things before moving on to the more specific edits.

Letting Elements Fly on Full Auto

The Auto fixes are like shooting with your camera in Program or Auto mode. You probably won't admit it, but every now and then it's good to let the camera, or in this case the program, do all the driving. Remember that there are two versions of Auto Smart Fix. Give it a try in the Organizer, and then switch to the Editor and use the slider version for more control.

Change the View with a Quick Crop

One thing that I like to do when I am out shooting is to leave a little extra room in my images. I call it shooting loose. The reason I do this is that I enjoy cropping my images in postproduction. I have found compositions that I never even dreamed of while shooting, and if I had cropped too tight in the camera, I would never have been able to change things up. Give the Crop tool a little love by doing a simple crop in the Organizer. Then use the Crop tool in the Quick tab of the Edit panel, and try rotating the image to straighten it.

Sharper Than You Think

Sharpening is one of those things that people tend to overdo when they start learning to process. I think it has something to do with the human eye's love of contrast and sharp-looking things. Try sharpening with Auto Sharpen in the Organizer. You may not even notice any change. Now take the image to the Editor. Change your view to 100% by clicking the Actual Pixels button above the toolbar. Now apply sharpening with the Sharpen slider in the Quick tab of the Edit panel.

Let's Paint the Sky Blue

Literally. The first time I tried this tool, I was hooked and started scouring my collection of photos to find more to play with. Actually, playing is a good thing, since the brush takes a little getting used to. So find a pale blue sky and start painting. Just remember these quick tips: The larger the brush the less accurate it becomes, so use the left and right bracket keys to change the brush size. Also, if you paint in an area that doesn't need it, hold down the Alt key (Option key on a Mac) and paint over the unwanted selection to remove it. And don't forget to try lowering the layer opacity in the Full tab of the Edit section when you are done.

Share your results with the book's Flickr group!

Join the group here: flickr.com/groups/elements_fromsnapshotstogreatshots

4

ISO 200
1/3200 sec.
f/4
24mm lens

Using Camera Raw

GET THE MOST OUT OF EVERY RAW IMAGE

Does your camera have a raw mode? Are you using it? If so, then you will be doing a large portion of your image processing in Adobe Camera Raw (ACR), the program inside Elements that is specifically for processing raw camera files. The good news is that ACR is simple to use, and the results can be pretty amazing. It's fair to say that once you are done processing your image in ACR, you may have very little left to do in the Editor.

The original image was a little crooked, so I used the Straighten tool on the grate behind the musicians.

I changed the White Balance setting to Shade and then adjusted it with the Temperature slider.

I really wanted the image to pop, so I gave it some over-the-top sharpening and a high setting on the Clarity slider.

ISO 1600
1/400 sec.
f/2.8
28mm lens

Shooting in the raw format can sometimes be challenging. It doesn't require any additional work on the camera end, but the processing can be more extensive. It can also challenge your memory, because the image you see on your computer will not necessarily look like it did when you shot it. The great thing is that you have complete control over everything that is done to the image, and when you are done, you can end up with something that is even better than you first imagined. This shot looked off-color, kind of blue, and a little crooked, but after a few minutes in Adobe Camera Raw, it really came to life.

The Camera Standard profile was the best option for proper color rendition and contrast.

WHY YOU SHOULD BE SHOOTING RAW

Your camera most likely has a choice of image formats for storing the pictures on the memory card. JPEG is probably the format that is most familiar to anyone who has been using a digital camera.

There is nothing wrong with JPEG if you are taking casual shots. JPEG files are ready to use right out of the camera. Why go through the process of adjusting raw images of the kids opening presents when you are just going to email them to Grandma? And JPEG is just fine for journalists and sports photographers who are shooting nine frames a second and who need small images to transmit across the wire. So what is wrong with JPEG? Absolutely nothing—unless you care about having complete creative control over all of your image data (as opposed to what a compression algorithm thinks is important).

Just to give you a little background, JPEG is not actually an image format. It is a compression standard, and compression is where things can go bad. When you have your camera set to JPEG—whether it is set to High or Low compression—you are telling the camera to process the image however it sees fit and then throw away enough image data to make it shrink into a smaller space. In doing so, you give up subtle image details that you will never get back in postprocessing. That is an awfully simplified statement, but it's still fairly accurate.

SO WHY RAW?

First and foremost, raw images are not compressed. (Some cameras have a compressed raw format, but it is lossless compression, which means there is no loss of actual image data.) Also, raw image files will require you to perform postprocessing on your photographs. This is not only necessary, it is the reason that most photographers use the raw format.

Raw images have a greater dynamic range than JPEG-processed images. This means that you can recover image detail in the highlights and shadows that just isn't available in JPEG-processed images.

A raw image is a 14-bit image, which means it contains more color information than a JPEG, which is almost always an 8-bit image. More color information means more to work with and smoother changes between tones—kind of like the difference between performing surgery with a scalpel as opposed to a butcher's knife. They'll both get the job done, but one will do less damage.

A raw image offers more control over sharpening, because you are the one who is applying it according to the effect you want to achieve. Once again, JPEG processing applies a standard amount of sharpening that you cannot change after the fact. Once it is done, it's done.

Finally, and most importantly, a raw file is your digital negative. No matter what you do to it, you won't change it unless you save your file in a different format. This means that you can come back to that raw file later and try different processing settings to achieve differing results and never harm the original image. By comparison, if you make a change to your JPEG and accidentally save the file, guess what? You have a new original file, and you will never get back to that first image. That alone should make you sit up and take notice.

USING ADOBE CAMERA RAW

To open your image in Adobe Camera Raw from the Organizer, select the image's thumbnail in the Media Browser and then click the Fix tab. Click Edit Photos. Elements will open the Editor and then open your image in Adobe Camera Raw. If you are already in the Editor, choose File > Open and then double-click the raw file you want to use.

THE CAMERA RAW ADJUSTMENT TOOLS

There are three tabs on the right side of the Adobe Camera Raw interface. Each one contains a variety of controls that enable you to make specific adjustments to your image. You will probably do most of your work in the Basic tab (**Figure 4.1**).

THE BASIC TAB

A raw image file contains no adjustments when it comes out of your camera. It does, however, contain the metadata that stores the camera settings used to create the image. This includes things like aperture, ISO, and shutter speed settings. It also has the camera's white balance information, which is what shows up in the White Balance control.

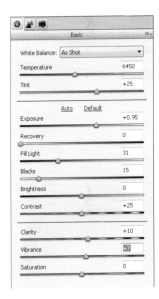

FIGURE 4.1
The Basic tab is where you will spend most of your time in Camera Raw.

FIGURE 4.2
Click the White Balance drop-down to find a better white balance or change the look of your photo.

GETTING THOSE COLORS RIGHT

The default White Balance setting is As Shot, but you can change that to several different presets, just as you would on your camera. Included in the list of presets are Auto, Daylight, Cloudy, Shade, Tungsten, Fluorescent, Flash, and Custom (**Figure 4.2**).

Selecting one of these presets will change the Temperature and Tint settings of the image to a preset value. If you do this manually by using one of the sliders below the White Balance presets, the White Balance setting will be set to Custom. If you have something in your image that is neutral in color, you can click on it with the White Balance tool and automatically adjust the white balance. This is also helpful if you have included a white balance card in one of your images.

If you have not included a white balance card in your image, start with a preset that closely matches the light that your photo was taken in. If it still needs a little adjusting, fine-tune it with the Temperature slider until it looks right. The goal of this adjustment is to remove any color cast in your image and make the colors look like they should.

MAKING TONAL CORRECTIONS WITH THE EXPOSURE SLIDER

Once you have adjusted the image's white balance, it's time to start correcting the overall brightness and darkness. A good reference for what to adjust can be found in the histogram in the upper-right corner of your screen. A histogram is a graphical representation of the tones in your photo, with the darkest areas on the left and the brightest parts on the right. If your image is overexposed or has areas that are so bright that they will appear as white and have no visual information, the histogram will have a spike on the right side. If there is a lot of black in the photo, the histogram will have a large spike on the left side. The key is to make sure that you have good tones throughout the image and that the blacks and whites are as accurate as possible. The easiest way to do this is by adjusting the Exposure sider.

If you need to make overall adjustments to the image brightness, you can do this by moving the Exposure slider, which has a default setting of zero. The adjustments are related to stops in exposure value. You can make the image four stops brighter by moving the slider to the right, or four stops darker by moving it to the left.

CHECK YOUR CLIPPING WARNINGS

If you look at the histogram, you will see triangles in the upper-left and upper-right corners of the graph. These are your clipping warning indicators. Clipping is when an area of the photo is either so dark or so light that it no longer contains any detail and appears as black or white in the photo. When this happens, the small triangles will turn white (**Figure 4.3**). If you want to get an idea of where the clipping is occurring in the photo, click the white triangle and a color overlay will appear on your image in the offending area (red for overexposed and blue for underexposed). Depending on the amount of clipping, you might be able to correct the exposure to get details back in your image.

FIGURE 4.3
The histogram is full of useful exposure information.

Remember that sometimes black is black and white is white. That is, there might be areas in your image that contain some clipping but do not need to be corrected. If you have the sun in your shot, no amount of image adjustment will get rid of the clipping warning, so decide just how much effort you need to apply to fixing the problem.

SAVING YOUR HIGHLIGHTS WITH THE RECOVERY TOOL

The Recovery slider is an amazing tool for fixing those areas in your photo that are too bright without having to make the rest of the image darker. As you move the Recovery slider to the right, the brightest parts of the photo will get darker and darker. The best way to use this tool is to watch the highlight clipping warning in the histogram. You can continue moving the Recovery slider to the right until the warning disappears. An easier way to do this is to click the highlight warning triangle and then move the Recovery slider to the right until the red overlay on the image disappears.

NOTE

You can quickly turn on the over- and underexposure warning overlays on your image by pressing the O key for over and the U key for under.

SEEING IN THE SHADOWS WITH THE FILL LIGHT SLIDER

If you have the opposite problem of too many dark areas with no detail, you can try using the Fill Light slider. Moving this slider to the right will lighten the darkest parts of your image without affecting the highlights. The slider can be adjusted to a setting of 100, but it usually isn't necessary to go more than 20 points to fix most problems.

BETTER-LOOKING BLACKS

As indicated earlier, raw images have no adjustments coming out of the camera, but they all need some corrections to make them look better. That's why the Blacks slider has a default setting of 5. This setting does a couple of things. First, it adds a little contrast to the image by raising the blackest part of the image. Second, it adds some saturation to colors. When you increase the black level, you are setting a new point for which tones will appear black in the image. The higher the number, the darker your shadows will appear. The Blacks slider does not have much effect on the middle or brightest tones in the image.

FINE-TUNING YOUR TONAL BRIGHTNESS

The Brightness slider is a lot like the Exposure slider in that it can make the image look darker or brighter. The difference is that the Exposure slider can clip the highlights or shadows, but when you move the Brightness slider to the right, it compresses the tones in the brightest parts while expanding the shadows.

The best way to use this slider is to first make your other tonal adjustments (Exposure, Recovery, Fill Light, and Blacks) and then adjust the Brightness slider as needed. It might be necessary to go back and make some minor adjustments to the other tonal sliders after adjusting the Brightness slider.

ADJUSTING IMAGE CONTRAST

The Contrast slider is set to 25 by default, and moving it to the right will increase contrast in your image. A contrast increase means that you will have an increase in the middle tones of the image, making them either darker or lighter. By lowering the adjustment (moving the slider to the left), you increase the middle tones by making dark areas lighter and light areas darker.

ADDING SOME VISUAL PUNCH WITH THE CLARITY SLIDER

Of all the sliders in the Camera Raw interface, the one that I always use is Clarity. This adjustment adds contrast to the midtones in a way that can punch up a dull image or soften one that looks too crisp. The default setting for this adjustment is zero, and moving it to the right will increase midtone contrast and make things look more crisp and snappy. Moving the slider into the negative numbers will decrease the midtone contrast and give things a softer look. This is a great way to improve the skin tones in a portrait. The best way to make the adjustments is to zoom your image to a 100% view so that you can better judge the effects of the slider.

BRIGHTENING DULL COLORS

The Vibrance slider is there to let you make adjustments to the less colorful parts of your image. By moving the slider to the right, the saturation of less colorful areas is increased without affecting the already saturated areas. The algorithm that controls the adjustment was written so that skin tones are not as affected by the increase of saturation. You can also get a more subtle palette of colors by reducing the vibrance of the image.

FROM BLACK AND WHITE TO CRAZY COLORS

If you want to give a boost to all the colors in your image, use the Saturation slider. Moving it to the right will increase the saturation of all colors in the image. Moving it to the left will decrease saturation all the way to the point of looking like a black and white image.

THE DETAIL TAB

The Detail tab contains two sections for improving your image. Every raw image needs some level of image sharpening and even noise reduction. Even if you are going to do additional work in the Elements Editor, it's still a good idea to spend a little time in this tab to make sure you are getting the best possible details in your photo (**Figure 4.4**).

FIGURE 4.4
Be sure to zoom in to 100% whenever you sharpen or reduce noise.

ALL RAW FILES NEED SHARPENING

When you click the Detail tab, you will see that some base sharpening has already been applied to your photo. That's because raw images do not have sharpening added by the camera, like JPEGs do, so Camera Raw adds a little bit to get you started. I prefer to sharpen my images twice during my workflow: the first time in Camera Raw and then once again in the Editor.

The first thing you should do is zoom in to a 100% view so that you can see the precise results of your sharpening efforts. Then, raise the Amount slider to a level that provides good detail to sharp edges in the image. The goal of sharpening is to make the edges look better without affecting the things that shouldn't be sharp, like the sky or skin or a flat surface. Typically, you will get the best results with the Amount slider somewhere between 50 and 100.

The Radius slider controls how much the sharpening extends out from the edges. The default setting is 1, and I leave it set there most of the time. If you have an image that looks sort of fuzzy, you can try raising this a little bit, but be careful not to go overboard.

The Details slider is set to 25 by default, and that is generally where I leave it. It can be raised if you want to increase small details, like intricate lines. When using this slider, be mindful of avoiding halos. Go too high on the Details slider and you will get contrast lines around your edges that can look like glowing halos. If you start seeing them, lower the Details slider until they go away.

The final slider in the Sharpening section is called Masking, and it is one of my favorites. It allows you to mask out or restrict the sharpening to only the edge areas of the image, while avoiding surfaces. Using the slider is as simple as moving it to the right, but it can be difficult to see the results, which is why I prefer to use a visual helper. Hold down the Alt (Option) key while dragging the slider, and a black and white mask will appear on the image in the preview window. At first, the window will appear completely white, but as you move the slider to the right you will see portions of the image turn black (**Figure 4.5**). Keep moving the slider until just the edges that you want sharpened are white and everything else is black.

If you aren't sure where to start with your Sharpening settings, try these: Amount 70, Radius 1.0, Detail 30, and Masking 70. Now move the sliders and fine-tune for your image. The important thing here is that you don't over-sharpen your photos. A sharp image with good details is great, but one that is over-sharpened will stick out like a sore thumb.

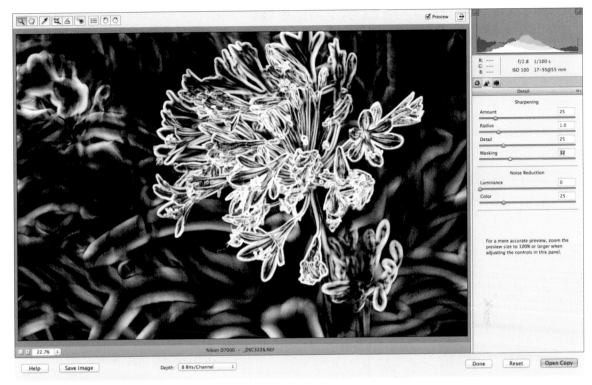

FIGURE 4.5
Hold down the Alt (Option) key when adjusting the sharpen mask to see only the areas you are masking.

TAMING THE NOISE

Sometimes it's necessary to shoot with a high ISO even though you know it will add digital noise to your image. When this happens, you can turn to the Noise Reduction sliders to help eliminate the problem. There are just two sliders in this section, Luminance and Color. Most noise you will encounter can be handled by adjusting the Luminance slider. All that's required is to move the slider to the right until the noise in your image is gone. Too much noise reduction can make your picture look soft, though, so don't overdo it. You might find that you need to readjust your Sharpening settings after applying noise reduction, but you can also add some sharpness back into the image once it is in the Editor.

The Color slider is set to a default of 25 and rarely needs to be adjusted. If you are still seeing small multicolored specks in your image, move the Color slider to the right until they are gone.

THE CAMERA CALIBRATION TAB

Have you ever looked at the image on your camera's LCD screen and thought, "Wow, this looks great!" and then when you get it in your computer it's a little disappointing? You have probably experienced this if you shoot raw, because the image you see on your camera is a JPEG that has been corrected and enhanced by the camera. But since you are working with a raw file, all of that is stripped away once you open it in the computer. A quick way to add back some of that pizzazz is to select a new camera profile from the Camera Calibration tab.

IMPROVING YOUR IMAGE WITH CAMERA PROFILES

Camera profiles are settings that attempt to match the camera manufacturer's colors in different shooting scenarios. The Adobe Standard profile is the default setting for all raw files. It is fairly generic and treats all raw files the same way no matter which camera produced them. It is simply a base enhancement to improve color rendering in the yellows, reds, and oranges of your image.

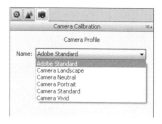

FIGURE 4.6
Camera profiles can dramatically change the look of your image.

The camera profiles are specific to your camera and often contain choices such as Camera Standard, Landscape, Vivid, Portrait, and Neutral, but they might be slightly different for your camera make and model (**Figure 4.6**).

Using the profiles is as easy as selecting a new profile from the drop-down menu. You will get an instant preview in the main preview window. Press the P key to toggle between before and after views.

There's no way of knowing which profile will look best, so it's best to try them all. I find I get the best results with the Landscape and Vivid profiles. They can be a little contrasty, though, so I don't necessarily use them all the time. It depends on the subject.

A FEW HANDY TOOLS

We have covered most of the image adjustment features in ACR, but there are some tools you should know about that will help make your editing easier. There is a toolbar at the top left of the ACR window. It contains the Zoom, Hand, Eyedropper, Crop, Straighten, Red Eye Removal, Preferences, and Rotate Image tools. Let's take a quick look at each of these tools and their specific functions (**Figure 4.7**).

FIGURE 4.7
The Camera Raw toolbar is in the upper-left corner of the workspace.

ZOOM, ZOOM

The Zoom tool's icon looks like a magnifying glass. Click it to select it, and then click on your image to zoom in. You can also click and drag to zoom in to a specific location. Holding down the Alt (Option) key while clicking will zoom back out of the image. If you double-click the Zoom tool icon, the magnification will be set to 100%.

THE HELPING HAND

The Hand tool allows you to move around the image when it is zoomed in. This can be handy when you are working at 100% and want to check your processing on different parts of the image. If you double-click the Hand tool icon, the image will zoom out to fit in the screen.

BETTER COLOR IN A CLICK

To get an accurate white balance in your image, especially if you have included a white balance card in your shot, you will want to use the Eyedropper tool (**Figure 4.8**). Its purpose is to set whatever color it is clicked on to neutral, which should then correct all the other colors in the image. It works better on medium to dark gray areas, so clicking something that is white or black may not render the desired results. For the most accurate white balance, you should take a photo of a neutral white balance card during your shoot to use as reference. In a pinch, you can grab a shot of some warm asphalt to use as a gray point for balancing your other photos.

FIGURE 4.8

The White Balance option can quickly correct colors when used with a white balance card.

CROP THE UNWANTED

The Crop tool functions very much like the Crop tool that we covered in Chapter 3. Just select the tool, and then click and drag a new crop. Adjust the crop window by dragging the corners. If you want to size the crop to a predetermined aspect ratio, click and hold the Crop tool icon in the toolbar. A drop-down menu will appear with several aspect ratios to choose from, as well as an option to clear the crop altogether. There's also an option to turn on the crop overlay, which will put rule-of-thirds guide marks on top of your crop window to help with the composition.

DRAW A LINE TO STRAIGHTEN THINGS UP

If your image contains vertical or horizontal lines, such as those in a building or the horizon, that you want to use as a guide for straightening, you can click the Straighten tool. Then simply click one edge of the straight line, drag across to the other end of your straight object, and let go (**Figure 4.9**). The image will automatically be straightened to the line you drew, as well as cropped to keep it squared up. Once you use it, you will instantly see what I am talking about.

GET THE RED OUT

The Red Eye Removal tool is another easy fix for an annoying problem. Just as you did with the Red Eye Removal tool in Chapter 3, select the tool, draw a box over the red eye, and watch it disappear. Everything should be so easy.

WHAT'S YOUR PREFERENCE?

There aren't too many preferences that you need to worry about in Adobe Camera Raw, but one thing you might consider is the Default Image Settings section. It contains three check boxes that let you apply some defaults when images are opened in the program (**Figure 4.10**). The "Apply auto tone adjustments" check box will automatically apply tone adjustments to every image that is opened. The other two check boxes relate to the defaults that are set in the Defaults menu. You can assign default settings to a specific camera serial number so that every time a raw file is opened from a particular camera, a set

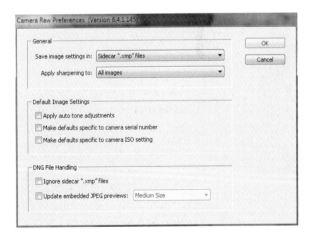

FIGURE 4.10
The Camera Raw Preferences dialog.

of default adjustments is applied. You can also do this for a specific ISO setting. This would be handy for setting default noise reduction for any image that was captured with an ISO of 1600, for example.

ROTATE (LEFT AND RIGHT)

Many of today's cameras have the ability to auto-rotate an image file depending on the orientation of the camera at the time the photo was taken. This rotation data is embedded in the metadata and then read by the software so that the image can be rotated to its appropriate orientation during viewing and editing. If, however, this is not the case with your camera, and your vertical images are displaying in a landscape orientation, you can click one of the Rotate Image tools to rotate 90 degrees to the left or right. It's not a necessity to do this, but I certainly find it easier to work on my images when they are facing the right way.

THE DEFAULTS MENU

In the Camera Raw interface, just to the right of the tabs title bar, is a small icon that lets you access the Defaults menu. When you click this icon, a pop-up menu appears with options that allow you to revert to the Camera Raw default settings, to the previous conversion settings, or even to custom settings. You can also create a new Camera Raw default for use with future images.

CREATING A CAMERA RAW DEFAULT

1. Open an image in Adobe Camera Raw.

2. Make all the adjustments that you want to apply as defaults to future images.

3. Click the Defaults menu icon, and select Save New Camera Raw Defaults from the pop-up menu (**Figure 4.11**).

The next time you open an image in ACR, your new defaults will be applied as a starting point for your processing.

FIGURE 4.11
You can set your current adjustments as new defaults in the Defaults menu.

Sometimes it's nice to set a default that you want to use for a large batch of images but not necessarily for all images for the rest of time. In this instance, you can set a new default and then once you are done with it, go to the Defaults menu and click the Reset Camera Raw Defaults option. This will set everything back to the Adobe defaults.

NOTE

The new default setting is best used if you find that you are applying the same settings to all of your images. So why not start off with those settings? Remember that a default is just a jumping-off point for your edits, so you don't want to change every adjustment setting, just those that would apply to all of your images, like Sharpening, Clarity, and maybe Camera Calibration.

WORKING WITH MULTIPLE IMAGES

Camera Raw is great for working with one image at a time, but you can also open a large group to speed up your workflow. This will allow you to apply adjustments to all of your images at once instead of opening each one individually. I use this feature all the time when I have taken the time to shoot a white balance card and want to apply the same white balance adjustment to all the photos from that shooting session.

OPENING MULTIPLE IMAGES IN ACR

1. Go to the Organizer and find the files that you want to use.
2. Select the images by Control/Command-clicking them or by clicking the first image and then Shift-clicking the last image in the group (**Figure 4.12**).

FIGURE 4.12

To open a group of images in Camera Raw, select them in the Organizer and then click the Edit Photos option.

3. Go to the Fix tab and click Edit Photos to open the Editor and send the selected images to Camera Raw.

4. When ACR opens, the images will appear in a filmstrip along the left side of the program. Click one to work on just that image.

5. To apply the same adjustment to all of the images simultaneously, click one thumbnail to make it the focused image.

6. Click the Select All button at the top of the filmstrip to activate changes to all of the images in the strip (**Figure 4.13**).

FIGURE 4.13
To make synchronized changes to all your images, click the Select All button at the top of the thumbnail section.

7. Once you are finished making synchronized adjustments to all the images, click a different thumbnail or use the Control-D (Command-D) keyboard shortcut to deselect the group.

Once you are done with your edits, you have a couple of choices. You can click the Select All button and then click the Open Images button at the lower-right corner of the screen to move all of the images from ACR to the Project Bin in the Editor. If you only want to take some of the images into the Editor, Control/Command-click the thumbnails to select them and then click the Open Images button. If you have only one image selected in ACR, you will notice that the Open Images button reads Open Image (singular), and only the selected image will be opened in the Editor.

Of course, you may have only wanted to work on the images in ACR without actually going to the Editor. If that is the case, click the Done button (in the lower-right corner of the screen), and ACR will save your raw edits and take you back to the Organizer. Notice that the image thumbnails in the Organizer have been updated to reflect the adjustments that you made in ACR.

OPENING JPEGS IN CAMERA RAW

You may find that after working with ACR you really enjoy the power and quickness of the edits and want to edit all of your images with it, including JPEGs. Well, you most certainly can do that, but you have to go about it a little differently than you would with raw files.

The default editor for raw images is ACR, so it opens by default when you go to the Editor. This isn't the case for JPEGs, so you will need to open them differently.

OPENING A JPEG IN ACR

1. Open the Editor without opening an image.

2. Choose File > Open As (**Figure 4.14**).

3. Locate the folder that contains the image that you want to open, and then select the file.

4. Select Camera Raw from the Open As drop-down menu (**Figure 4.15**).

5. Click the Open button.

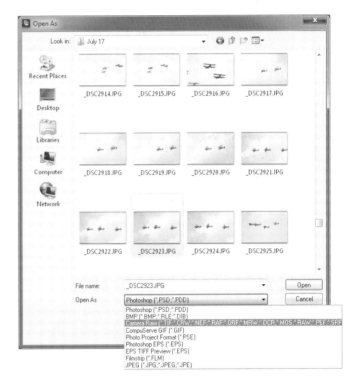

FIGURE 4.14
To open a JPEG in Camera Raw, go to the File menu in the Editor and select Open As.

FIGURE 4.15
Be sure to select Camera Raw from the Open As drop-down menu.

You will now have access to most of the features in ACR for editing your image. A few things will be different, because of the differences between JPEGs and raw image files.

First, there are no custom camera profiles. Instead, ACR will use the embedded profile in the file. You will also find that there is no longer a large group of white balance options to choose from. When you click the White Balance drop-down menu, you will only see As Shot, Auto, and Custom. You can, however, use the White Balance tool to click-balance your images using a neutral color in the photo, and you can make adjustments using the Temperature and Tint sliders.

Remember that even though you can open a JPEG in ACR, you will have limited results compared to a raw file. JPEGs have much less exposure information and dynamic range than raw files.

MY CAMERA RAW WORKFLOW

It can be confusing trying to figure out what to do first to an image in Camera Raw. There isn't really a proper order for the way things should be done, and over time you will develop your own workflow. Until then, here's my ordered workflow for you to follow along with.

STEP BY STEP

1. Open the image in ACR, and go to the Camera Calibration tab.
2. Select the camera profile that is most fitting for your image.
3. Jump to the Basic tab and adjust the white balance if necessary.
4. Check the clipping warnings to see if there are any problems with the high-lights. If so, adjust the Recovery slider.
5. If there are large areas of clipped shadows that are important to the image, use the Fill Light slider to brighten them.
6. Increase the Blacks setting a little to improve contrast and saturation.
7. Increase the Clarity setting (about 15 to 30 points) and the Vibrance setting.
8. Finally, go to the Details tab, zoom in to 100%, and adjust the Sharpening settings.

Of course, some of these adjustments have an effect other adjustments, so I often go back and tweak some of the previous steps. For instance, raising the Blacks slider can make the image dark, so I might use the Exposure or Brightness slider to lighten things up a little. Just remember that every image is a little different, so be flexible with your edits.

Chapter 4 Assignments

The best thing to do with Adobe Camera Raw is just play with it and get to know what all the adjustments can do for your image. This might be a problem, though, if you have yet to shoot any raw images. You could use a JPEG, but you really should use raw files to get an idea of all the features. That's why I am including a few of my raw files in the bonus materials for you to play with (see Introduction). Just download the files and import them into the Organizer to get started.

Get that JPEG Look in Your Raw Files

The camera profiles can have a huge impact on how your images look. Generally speaking, they can make them look just like they did on the camera LCD screen when you took them. Open your file in ACR, and then try some different camera profiles in the Camera Calibration tab.

Back to Basics

The majority of your processing work will be done in the Basic tab. Spend a little time getting to know the sliders and adjustments here. Try clicking the clipping warnings to see the overlays, and then use the Recovery and Fill Light sliders to make the overlays go away.

Sharpen Like a Pro

One of the coolest and most useful features of the Sharpening tools is the mask overlay. Masking the sharpening to only the edges, rather than sharpening everything, will give your images a much more polished look. Apply some sharpening to the image, and then hold the Alt (Option) key and move the Masking slider to apply sharpening just where you want it.

Crop and Straighten

Cropping and straightening work hand in hand. When you straighten an image, you also crop it, because the image is being slightly rotated. Use the Straighten tool to straighten out a line or horizon in an image, and then click the Crop tool to adjust the crop composition.

Share your results with the book's Flickr group!

Join the group here: flickr.com/groups/elements_fromsnapshotstogreatshots

5

ISO 400
1/160 sec.
f/9
11mm lens

Using the Elements Editor

MOVING PAST THE AUTOMATIC FEATURES AND GUIDES

Up to this point, we have covered simple editing features in Elements that allow you to do some basic enhancements. Now it's time to start digging in to the Editor function of the program so that you can take more control over your image processing. Image processing in Elements can be compared to taking pictures with a digital SLR camera. You can depend on the automatic settings to create a photograph, but the camera doesn't know what you want—only what it's programmed to do. To obtain more creative results, you have to abandon the automatic modes and start taking control of the picture-taking process. The same can be said for image processing in Elements. There are a lot of automatic tools, many that we have already covered, that can instantly improve the look of your photograph. But once again, the program doesn't know what it is looking at and can therefore only make educated guesses about how to best process your image. To really make that photograph look like you want, you will need to take control by using the tools in the Editor.

PORING OVER THE PICTURE

To open up the shadows,
I adjusted the Fill Light
slider during the Camera
Raw processing.

Shade can sometimes create
a flat-looking image, so I
used a Levels adjustment to
increase the contrast.

ISO 200
1/25 sec.
f/9
120mm lens

There was a little too much foreground in the original file, so I used the Crop tool to tighten up the composition.

The moss was a major character in the image, so I used the Vibrance slider to make it really colorful.

I found this shot while wandering around the ruins of Angkor Wat in Cambodia a few years ago. It was away from the beaten path and the crush of the crowds in a quiet, tree-shaded spot. I wasn't sure if it was a burial plot because it was unlike the cemeteries I had seen in other locations, but the markers did remind me of tombstones. There was a symmetry to the spot that, combined with the brightly colored moss, made for a great shot.

TOOLS TO BRING YOUR PHOTOS TO LIFE

Sometimes it doesn't take much to breathe life into an image. It may be lacking contrast, or perhaps it needs color correction. It could be lacking good composition that would be cured by a new crop. And what image doesn't need the proper amount of sharpening to make it pop? In this chapter, we will begin working with some basic image adjustments and tools that will be the backbone of our image processing. But before we dive in to the deep end, let's check out some preferences that will give some behind-the-scenes help in our processing.

A QUICK HISTORY LESSON

Believe it or not, some people have never looked at the program preferences. That's a shame, because they are full of options that not only control how things are done in the Editor, but also let us work faster and smarter. Take the History & Cache options (**Figure 5.1**). The default History States setting is 50. This means that you can perform 50 operations in the Editor and then undo them. It also means that Elements is going to dedicate a large amount of memory remembering each state of the image prior to every one of those 50 operations. This is actually overkill. I rarely need more than 20 history states, so let's start with lowering it to 20.

FIGURE 5.1
The History States preference is in the Performance section.

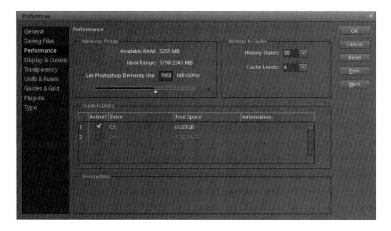

1. Choose Edit > Preferences > Performance.
2. In the History & Cache section, double-click in the text box that reads 50.
3. Type in 20, and then click outside the box.

You can click the OK button to set the history states, but as long as we have the box open, why not check out a few more options that might be helpful to change?

RECENT FILE LIST

There is a list in the File menu that lets you quickly access the last 10 documents that you had open in the Editor. I usually change this to 20 (**Figure 5.2**). I just prefer to have more of them so that I have quick access to a longer list of my recent edits.

FIGURE 5.2
You can increase the number of remembered files in the Saving Files section of the preferences.

The Recent File list is near the bottom of the Saving Files section of the Preferences box. You can quickly access the different sections of the Preferences dialog by clicking the appropriate heading on the left side.

BE PRECISE

There are a few tools that are used to either paint on the image or click in a specific location to do things like selecting a color or setting the white balance. The default setting for the brush tool is a circle, which will depict the shape and size of the brush so that you can accurately paint on your image. This works great for painting, but when it comes to accurately selecting a color with the Eyedropper tool, it is much more helpful to use a precise crosshair rather than an icon shaped like an eyedropper. To make this change, go to the Display & Cursors section and change the Other Cursors option from Standard to Precise (**Figure 5.3**).

FIGURE 5.3
You can change the
cursor type in the
Display & Cursors
section.

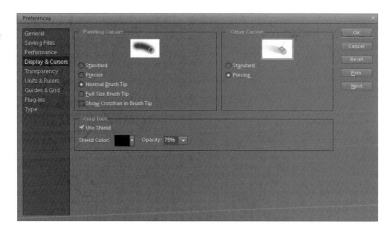

SET YOUR DOCUMENTS FREE

You may have noticed that when you open an image in the Editor, it is bound to the work area. You can release it from the boundaries by changing a setting in the General preferences section. In the Options section of the General tab, select the Allow Floating Documents in Full Edit Mode check box (**Figure 5.4**). That will remove the restriction of having your image bound to the work area. It will now be in a floating window that can be resized and moved around your workspace (**Figure 5.5**). To move the image around, click and hold its title bar while moving. If you want to resize, drag one of the lower corners. To re-dock the image to the workspace, drag it to the top of the workspace window until a blue line outlines the workspace and then let go. It will snap right into the window. To undock, drag the smaller title bar away from the window.

FIGURE 5.4
Selecting the Allow
Floating Docu-
ments in Full Edit
Mode check box
will let you move
your image boxes
around.

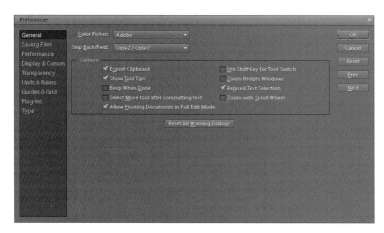

FIGURE 5.5
An image residing
in its own image
window in the
Editor.

There are a lot of other preferences that can be tweaked to your liking, but I would advise you to use the program for a while before changing the rest of them. If something isn't to your liking, such as the unit of measurement or the color of the line used to create a guide, then go back in and change it. And don't worry too much, because you can always click the Reset button to set things back to their defaults.

OPENING YOUR WORK

If you have been working with the Organizer, you already know how to open an image from there, but it's not necessary. You can, in fact, open images directly from within the Editor. Choose File > Open. This will open a new dialog, where you can select the file or files that you would like to work on (**Figure 5.6**). The dialog looks similar to the Windows Explorer window, or the Finder window on a Mac, and allows you to navigate to the drive and folder of your choice and then click an image file to open it. If you happen to have various file types in the folder, you can select one of the many image file types from the Files of Type drop-down menu. This will restrict the files shown in the window to only that selected type. Once you've selected a file, click the Open button to return to the Editor and begin working on the image.

SAVE EARLY AND OFTEN

Saving your files is as simple as choosing File > Save, but there are a few things you should know first so that you can save properly and possibly save yourself a few headaches down the road. First of all, Elements will want to save your file whenever you have made any change to it at all. It will tell you this by throwing up a reminder screen when you try to close your image (**Figure 5.7**). For the moment, let's assume that you have been working on a JPEG file in the Editor. It's very important that you realize that any changes that you have made to that file will be saved to the original, making the edited version the new original. This is why it's very important that you are OK with losing the original image. If you want to maintain the original JPEG, you will need to perform a Save As instead of a Save.

FIGURE 5.7
If you make any change to an image, you will be prompted to save.

Save As lets you choose a new name or location for the edited file that will not overwrite the original. For example, if I am working on a file named DSC_7722.jpg and I make some edits, I can go to the File menu and select Save As. Then, in the Save As dialog, I can select a new location and file name. By default, the Editor will rename my image by adding the word "edited" to the file name. It will also default to the folder that the image originated from (**Figure 5.8**).

FIGURE 5.8
The Save As dialog.

You can also choose from several save options, such as including the edited image in the Organizer, saving it in a version set with the original, saving as a copy, and including an ICC profile. I prefer to make copies of my edited JPEG images rather than just doing a Save, so that I can always refer back to that original. It's not a requirement; it's just something that I do in my workflow. It probably has to do with the fact that raw images, which I shoot the majority of the time, are always saved as a copy since the raw file can't be overwritten.

That's one of the great things about shooting raw; you always have the original that you can edit over and over again without fear of having it damaged by saving. Also, since it can't be overwritten, you don't have to select Save As from the File menu. The default for raw files *is* Save As, and even if you select File > Save, it will open the Save As dialog with all the same options discussed above.

Another great thing about the Save As command is that you can create a completely new image file type depending on your needs. If you need an uncompressed file type, you can select TIFF or PSD, which is Adobe's proprietary file type. These two file types are really great if you have created a layered document (to be covered in

Chapter 6) and need to preserve the layers for possible future changes (**Figure 5.9**). You can also save your image as a PDF (Portable Document Format) file, which can be opened using Adobe Acrobat Reader.

FIGURE 5.9
Save As allows you to change the image file format to preserve layers.

NOTE

Non-compressed formats can be quite large and take up a lot of hard drive space. To find out how large your image would be in an uncompressed format, click the fly-out menu in the lower-left corner of the image editing area and select Document Sizes (**Figure 5.10**). This will display the size of the image in terms of computer storage and give you an idea of how much space your image will take up in an uncompressed image format.

FIGURE 5.10
Click the fly-out menu to select the image info that will be displayed.

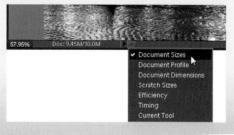

CROPPING FOR BETTER COMPOSITION

Now that we have set up the Editor and have a good idea of how to open and save our files, it's time to start making some meaningful edits. One of the first things I like to do is crop my images to help the composition and improve the overall aesthetics. Cropping is a very powerful function because it lets you determine what information will be left in the photo and what will be excluded. You can get creative by simply moving the crop window around on your photo and finding what works best. It's almost like working with the camera again, giving you a second chance to re-frame things for the perfect look.

FIGURE 5.11
There was too much boring sky in the top of the image.

In **Figure 5.11**, I had too much blue sky in the top of the image. The area near the top of the sky was a little boring and distracted from the main subject: the sandstone arch and mountains. By cropping with the same aspect ratio (4x6) as the original, I was able to remove the boring section of sky and keep the more interesting clouds (**Figure 5.12**). I used the rule-of-thirds crop overlay to position the crop to the left for more emphasis on the sandstone.

With the Crop tool, it's easy to find a new photo inside an existing image. I took the photograph of this bakery sign with a horizontal camera position (**Figure 5.13**). At the time, it looked to be the best angle. After I opened it in Elements, I was disappointed with the way the sign was leaning over to the right. The first thing I tried was rotating the entire image counterclockwise by choosing

FIGURE 5.12
After cropping, the composition is greatly improved, putting more emphasis on the arch.

Image > Rotate > 90° Left (**Figure 5.14**). This was an improvement, but the fire escape was still cluttering the top, so I clicked the Crop tool in the toolbar and drew out a crop over the image (**Figure 5.15**). I rotated the crop guide by putting the mouse cursor on a corner of the crop and dragging it a little to the left (**Figure 5.16**). Finally, I clicked the check mark at the bottom of the crop window to finalize my crop selection. You can see in **Figure 5.17** that rotating and cropping transformed the image into something better.

FIGURE 5.13
The original image suffers from poor composition.

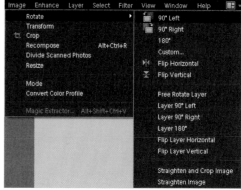

FIGURE 5.14
Image rotation tools can be found in the Image menu.

FIGURE 5.15
After rotating, a new crop was created for the sign.

FIGURE 5.16
Dragging a corner of the crop guide allows the crop to be rotated.

FIGURE 5.17
A completely new
and much-improved
image, thanks to
the Crop tool.

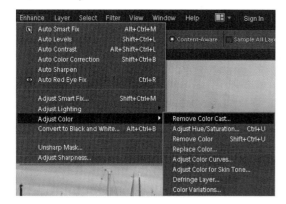

FIGURE 5.18
The Remove Color Cast tool is in the Enhance menu.

FIGURE 5.19
Click a neutral-color object to remove an unwanted color cast.

CORRECTING COLOR

A very common problem found in photos is color cast. A color cast normally occurs when there is an overall hue shift that is created by atmospheric conditions. For example, if you photograph something that is in the shade but there are blue skies overhead, you might see a slightly bluish cast to your photo, even though you had the white balance set correctly. It's not something that you normally see while shooting, because your eyes adjust for it. If you do have a slight color cast, you can use the Remove Color Cast tool to neutralize it and shift all the colors back to their normal hues. This tool works best if you have something in your image that is neutral and gray, but black or white can work if they are not clipped. Choose Enhance > Adjust Color > Remove Color Cast (**Figure 5.18**). A small helper box will pop up, and your mouse cursor will turn into an eyedropper icon (or a small crosshair if you changed the preference to the Precise option). Simply click it on neutral areas around your photo until you are happy with the color adjustment, and then click the OK button (**Figure 5.19**).

VARIATIONS

Of course, sometimes you might want to make color adjustments for artistic purposes. One of my favorite tools for this is called Color Variations. To use the tool, choose Enhance > Adjust Color > Color Variations. A dialog will open, displaying thumbnails with differing color variations (**Figure 5.20**). All you need to do is adjust the slider that determines the intensity of the color adjustment and then click the thumbnails to apply the change. The new color adjustment will display in the After box alongside the original so that you can compare the two. If you want more color, just click another color thumbnail. You can add or subtract colors to get just the look you want. In **Figure 5.21**, I warmed the image significantly by clicking the Decrease Blue button, which actually makes things look more yellow. I also added a vignette to the edge to give the image a bit of an antique look.

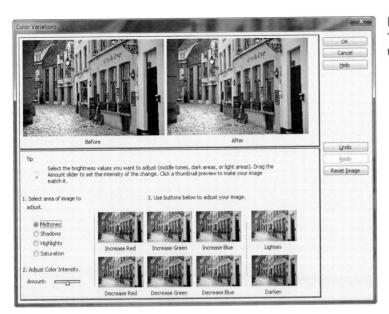

FIGURE 5.20
The Color Varia-
tions dialog.

FIGURE 5.21
The warmer color
and vignette gives
the image an Old
Country feel.

ADDING CONTRAST FOR MORE IMPACT

One way to add significant visual impact to an image is to increase the contrast. The human eye is naturally drawn to higher-contrast areas, so the simple act of increasing the difference between the lighter and darker parts of the image can go a long way toward improving a photo. There are several methods for increasing contrast, so let's start with the easiest.

BRIGHTNESS AND CONTRAST

This tool has been around since the first version of Elements, but it doesn't always get as much love as it deserves. That's probably because it wasn't always that great a tool. That is no longer the case, and the Contrast slider has been much improved

FIGURE 5.22
Brightness/Contrast is a simple tool that can add visual impact.

over the years. Its beauty is in its simplicity. Move the slider to the right and your contrast increases; move it left and it decreases (**Figure 5.22**). The key here is that the increase in contrast is more controlled now, and it does a great job of not clipping the darkest and lightest areas. It also keeps color shifts under control, which used to be one of the big complaints about the tool. To use the tool, choose Enhance > Adjust Lighting > Brightness/Contrast. Try using the tool in conjunction with the Brightness slider for a fast and efficient way to punch up an image.

CONTROL MIDTONE BRIGHTNESS WITH LEVELS

Another old-school adjustment tool for contrast is called Levels. It is simple in its application but has a little more power than the Contrast slider. That's because it lets you adjust the black and white points in your image and then decide where the middle tones should be (either darker or lighter). Another great feature of the Levels adjustment is that you can use it to correct color shifts in addition to contrast.

To make adjustments with the Levels tool, choose Enhance > Adjust Lighting > Levels or use the keyboard shortcut Control-L (Command-L). When the dialog opens, you will see a histogram representing the tones in your image along with three small triangles underneath, which can be moved to change the image contrast. Moving the black slider to the right will shift the darker tones to black. Moving the white triangle to the left will brighten the light tones, shifting them to white. The gray triangle adjusts the midtones; move it left to brighten and right to darken.

Another easy method of using the Levels adjustment is to use the three eyedroppers located under the Auto button. Click the black dropper to activate it and then click an area of the image that you want to set as black. Then activate the white dropper and click an area that should be white. Finally, use the gray dropper to click a middle gray tone (**Figure 5.23**). You have to be careful with the eyedroppers, though, because if you click something that has a color other than neutral, it will shift the colors in the image. After using the droppers, you can fine-tune your adjustments with the triangular sliders. We will explore Levels adjustments more in the next chapter.

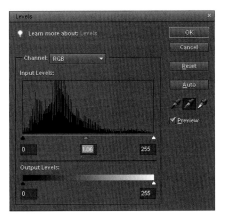

FIGURE 5.23
Using the gray eyedropper inside of Levels to color-correct the image.

CONTRAST ON A CURVE

The last contrast tool that we will look at is called Adjust Color Curves. I'm not sure why it has that name, because it has nothing to do with color and everything to do with image contrast. To use the tool, choose Enhance > Adjust Color > Adjust Color Curves. You will notice three areas in the dialog. At the top is a Before and After section that lets you actively monitor the changes to your image and compare them with the original. The section at the bottom left is where you select a style, but I prefer to think of them as presets. To the right of the styles are adjustment sliders to fine-tune your image.

I like this tool because it allows for the adjustment of midtone brightness and shadows, whereas the Levels adjustment has only one midtone adjustment. By allowing you to control four points of contrast, you can exercise far greater control over your image (**Figure 5.24**). To use the Adjust Color Curves adjustment, click one of the Select a Style presets and then move the sliders to refine the adjustment. When you are satisfied, click the OK button.

FIGURE 5.24
Adjust Color Curves
will give you more
control over subtle
midtone contrast
adjustments.

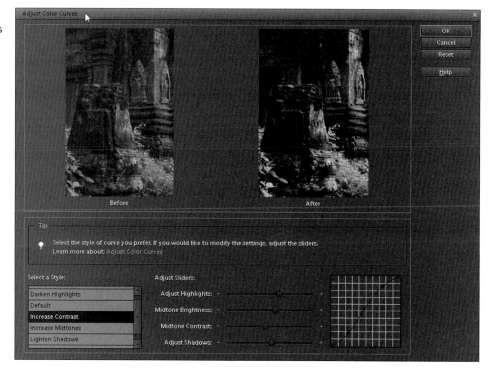

ADDING SHARPNESS

Sharpening is a necessary process no matter how you plan to use your photos. Generally speaking, there are just two different purposes for an image: electronic and printed. Think about it for a minute. If you take a picture, there are very limited options for how that image will end up. One option is to print it and the other is to use it on the computer (e.g., as an email attachment, a Web document, or even wallpaper).

These two purposes require different levels of sharpening because of the nature of the devices. A printed image requires much more sharpening than one that will stay on the computer. Ink from a printer has a tendency to spread out on paper, causing edges to look a little softer. Also, printed images can far exceed the size of any computer screen. Images viewed on a monitor don't require as much sharpening because they are typically viewed at much smaller sizes. Consider how much of your image is not visible when you zoom in to 100%—usually quite a bit. This means that you almost never view it at full resolution. Even so, it still requires some sharpening, especially if you reduce the file size.

ADJUST SHARPNESS

There are two different sharpening tools in the Enhance menu. The first is called Adjust Sharpness and can be found by choosing Enhance > Adjust Sharpness. It is a fairly simple tool with just two adjustment sliders, one for sharpness and the other for radius (**Figure 5.25**). The Amount slider increases the contrast of an edge. As you increase the amount, you are increasing the amount of contrast. The Radius slider controls how far out from the edge the contrast change will take effect. Raising the radius too much can create halos, so only use as much as necessary. If you start to see a bright halo along edges, decrease the radius. I typically use 1.0 to 1.2 pixels for my Radius setting.

FIGURE 5.25
Using the Adjust Sharpness tool.

The Remove option allows you to address different types of softness in your photos, such as lens and motion blur. I usually leave this setting on Gaussian Blur. The More Refined check box tells the tool to look at more subtle edges when sharpening rather than just the obvious hard edges. If you are looking for more detail in textured areas of an image, select this check box; otherwise, you can leave it alone.

FIGURE 5.26
The controls of the Unsharp
Mask tool.

UNSHARP MASK

Unsharp Mask is probably the most-used sharpening tool. It is similar to the Adjust Sharpness tool in that it uses an Amount slider to control the edge contrast, and a Radius slider for how far out from the edges the sharpening occurs. The big difference is that the Unsharp Mask tool has a Threshold slider for controlling how the sharpness is applied (**Figure 5.26**). The threshold determines the difference in value between pixels from those in surrounding areas. The higher the number, the less sharpening is applied. If the Threshold setting is left at zero, all of the pixels in the image will be sharpened. I think of the Threshold adjustment as a fade for the sharpening effect.

The important thing to remember when sharpening is to view images at the proper enlargement factor when applying the sharpen effect. If you are going to print a full-size image, zoom in to 100%. Also, I resize my images before applying any sharpening to avoid having to do it more than once.

Chapter 5 Assignments

Create Something New with a Crop

Cropping is a great exercise in being able to compose a strong image. Sure, it has practical purposes like straightening a photo or eliminating unwanted items along the edges, but it is also a great creative tool. Open some photos and then use the Crop tool to discover a new image inside the old one. This will also build your compositional skills, which will help when you are actually taking pictures.

Variations Are the Spice of Life

Well, maybe not life, but they can help you with a variety of choices when you're correcting color or trying to be creative. Use the Color Variations tool to sample some new color creativity in your image.

Sometimes Simple Is Good

As I said earlier in the chapter, the Brightness/Contrast tool does not get much respect in the retouching world, but it is actually a refined tool that can improve the look of an image with just a couple of quick slider movements. Find a dull image in your collection and see what a little contrast can do for you.

Take Your Images to New Levels (Adjustments)

The Levels adjustment looks simple on the surface, but it can be a very powerful tool. We will make much more use of it in the next chapter, so take some time to get used to all of the controls and how they can be used for adding contrast and correcting colors.

Share your results with the book's Flickr group!

Join the group here: flickr.com/groups/elements_fromsnapshotstogreatshots

6

ISO 200
1/1000 sec.
f/2.8
70mm lens

Local Edits

FIXING AND ENHANCING ISOLATED AREAS

Up to this point, we have concentrated on global image processes. By that I mean things that affect the image in its entirety, like color, contrast, and sharpness. Those are all essential skills, but what if there is a smaller area of the image that needs fixing? That's where selections, masks, and layers can really come in handy. There are also specialized tools that help fix little problems such as dust and unwanted items in your image. This is where we start moving from casual image fixer to retouching pro, and it's easier than you might think.

PORING OVER THE PICTURE

The White Balance setting was changed to Sunny and then warmed slightly using the Temperature slider.

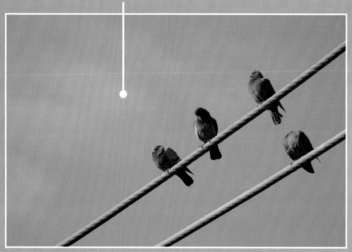

I wasn't planning to photograph pigeons when I went to the zoo. In fact, I had hoped to see some orangutans climbing across these wires. Instead, I saw these birds warming themselves in the afternoon sun. I quickly framed a shot and then went about my business. When I downloaded the photos, I noticed that the single bird on the lower wire was tucking in his head so far that he looked headless. No worries, though. I just grabbed the Clone Stamp tool, picked a good source location, and then there were three.

A Clarity adjustment made the details in the wires stand out.

ISO 200
1/1000 sec.
f/5.6
400mm lens

I used the Unsharp Mask
tool to sharpen the
image and gain definition
in the bird's feathers.

I used the Clone Stamp
tool to remove the bird
on the bottom wire.

THE LITTLE THINGS

My good friend and Adobe Photoshop instructor Scott Kelby is often asked what he fixes first in an image. His answer is pretty simple: whatever is bugging him the most. I guess that can be said for me as well, and the things that usually bother me the most are dust, blemishes, and stray hairs. Luckily, there are many tools that can make quick work of removing these problems and more.

SPOT HEALING BRUSH

One of the most useful tools to show up in Elements in quite some time is the Spot Healing Brush tool. This little gem removes dust spots, blemishes, and other small annoyances in your images, and it is very simple to use. First, click the tool in the tool-bar. It's the one that looks like a small bandage covering a dashed circle (**Figure 6.1**). There are settings for the brush in the top of the image frame that let you adjust how the brush works. I use the default type of healing, which uses the Content-Aware feature to fix the location where the brush is applied. Rather than using the brush size control, I use the left and right bracket keys to change the size of the brush, making it just larger than the item I want to get rid of. Using the brush is as easy as finding a dust spot and then clicking the brush on it. The Content-Aware feature will look at the surrounding pixels and then fill in the area with a perfect match.

FIGURE 6.1
Using the Spot Healing Brush tool is a quick way to get rid of dust spots in your image.

The one place the brush does not always function well is along contrast lines. So if you are trying to remove a dust spot or item along an edge and the Spot Healing Brush tool is acting up, you might give the Clone Stamp tool a try.

CLONE STAMP

Until the arrival of the healing tools, the Clone Stamp tool ruled the roost for removing little problems. It was also pretty handy at adding that third eyeball to the photo of your friend. The key to the Clone Stamp tool is picking the right clone location. In essence, you will be painting in one area of the image with pixels from another area. This is why you have to select a source for your pixels prior to cloning. To do that, activate the tool in the toolbar by clicking its icon (or pressing the S key), then hold down the Alt (Option) key and click a location where you want the pixels to come from.

When you move the brush away from the source location, you should see that the brush looks like it is filled with a floating image of the source locale. This is very handy for lining up areas where your cloning will cross a line or pattern, such as in **Figure 6.2**. The bird on the wire was hiding its head, so it was a good candidate for removal. The source location was selected further down the line and then lined up over the area where the bird was to be removed. When it was done, there was nothing left but a seamless wire (**Figure 6.3**).

PROTECTING AN AREA WITH SELECTIONS

In earlier chapters, we briefly discussed selections as tools that select and isolate parts of an image. But selections can also be helpful in protecting parts of an image from cloning and other actions. When you select part of an image, only the selected area is affected by your edits. That means you can paint, apply filters, adjust colors, and even clone stamp without messing up the unselected

FIGURE 6.2
By properly aligning the source pixels, the Clone Stamp tool can easily erase the bird from the wire.

FIGURE 6.3
After a successful clone job, the fourth bird is completely gone.

portion of the image. Look at **Figure 6.4**. The antennas on the ridgeline were ruining the shot, but it's an easy fix with the Clone Stamp tool. I used the Quick Selection tool to select the sky around the antenna but not the mountains. Then it was easy enough to select a source area for the Clone Stamp tool and paint away the antenna. Even when the brush happened to go over the mountain, it did not get cloned, because it was outside the selection area.

FIGURE 6.4
A selection keeps
the effect of the
Clone Stamp tool
confined to the sky
and protects the
mountains.

Of course, there are many selection tools that you can use, and you should choose the one that makes it easiest for you to get the job done.

A QUICK SELECTION LESSON

Using selections will be an integral part of your editing process, so let's take a quick look at all the tools.

THE MARQUEE TOOLS

Pressing the letter M on your keyboard will automatically switch you to the Rectangular and Elliptical Marquee tools. Press M or click and hold the icon in the toolbar to switch between the two. To use the tool, click and drag on your image. The shape and size will be determined by how far and in what direction you dragged the cursor (**Figure 6.5**). You can constrain the shape and size by adding some keyboard keys to the process. Hold down the Alt (Option) key to drag from the center out. Hold the Shift key while dragging to constrain the selection to a perfect circle or square. If you hold both the Shift and Alt (Option) keys while dragging, you will draw a perfect square or circle from the center out.

FIGURE 6.5
Selections made with the Rectangular and Elliptical Marquee tools.

If you want to add an additional area to the selection, hold down the Shift key (you should see a small + sign next to the mouse cursor). Holding the Alt (Option) key lets you subtract from a selection. These two functions only work once you have already established a selection onscreen. The *add* and *subtract* functions also work with other selection tools.

THE LASSO TOOLS

The Marquee tools are generally used for selecting larger areas and are not very accurate for selecting an edge or precise area. You can get more accurate selections by using the Lasso tools. Press the letter L on the keyboard to cycle through the three different Lasso tools. The standard Lasso tool will let you draw a selection freehand (**Figure 6.6**). Just click and draw. The only catch is that you have to keep the mouse button down the entire time you are drawing the selection. If you let go of the mouse button, the selection line will snap back to the point from which you began drawing. To finish a selection, you must end where you began.

FIGURE 6.6
A loose selection created with the Lasso tool.

FIGURE 6.7
A selection created with the Polygonal Lasso tool.

FIGURE 6.8
The Magnetic Lasso tool created a much more defined selection of the plane.

The Polygonal Lasso tool draws a series of straight, connected lines that you can use to select objects with straight edges, like buildings (**Figure 6.7**). Just click and drag out a line segment while holding down the mouse button. Let go of the button to complete a segment and then click and draw another. Do this until you end up back where you began.

The final tool in this group is the Magnetic Lasso. It likes to follow contrast edges and is pretty good at selecting objects photographed against a plain background. Simply click an edge and then follow along as the selection snaps to the edge (**Figure 6.8**). As you draw, the tool will lay down anchor points. If things start to go off track, press the Delete key to remove the last anchor point and continue from there. You can also click the mouse to add your own anchor points in tricky areas. Your selection will be completed when you arrive back at your starting point.

You can use these tools individually or together to add or subtract from a selection.

MAGIC WAND

If you need to select areas of your photo that are similar in color and tone, you can try using the Magic Wand tool. It has a Tolerance slider in the options bar that lets you control how much difference you want to allow between the pixel you clicked on and the ones surrounding it (**Figure 6.9**). A zero tolerance will select only pixels of the exact same color and tonality, whereas a setting of 32 is much more forgiving and allows for a larger selection. You can also choose whether to constrain the selection to only contiguous pixels (those that touch each other). If you turn off the contiguous option, pixels of similar color and tonality will be selected no matter where they are in the image.

FIGURE 6.9
The Magic Wand tool is handy for selecting large areas of similar color and brightness.

To use the tool, press W to make it active and then click the area that you want selected. Hold down the Shift key to add areas to your selection; hold down the Alt (Option) key to subtract areas from it.

QUICK SELECTION

We have already covered the Quick Selection tool, but to recap, use it to paint on the area that you want selected and it will automatically snap to edges. Adjust the brush size to increase accuracy in small areas. The brush automatically adds to the selection with each click, so hold the Alt (Option) key while painting to deselect an area.

To paint your selection without the auto-enhancing abilities of the Quick Selection tool, use the Selection Brush tool. Press the A key to cycle through to the Selection Brush tool, choose the brush diameter by using the bracket keys, and begin painting your selection.

SELECTION TIPS

Knowing how to use the selection tools is key to fixing specific portions of your image, but there are some related tips and tricks that will help you take full advantage of their power and help you move through your edits more quickly.

FIGURE 6.10
The Quick Selection tool is the fastest and most accurate method for selecting objects.

FIGURE 6.11
By inverting the selection, the bird can be isolated and then copied to a new layer.

FIGURE 6.12
Accessing the Refine Edge tool from the Select menu.

KEYBOARD SHORTCUTS

Knowing how to select is important, but deselecting is also a good thing to know. When you are done working with a selection, use the keyboard shortcut Control-D (Command-D) to deactivate it. To select your entire image, press Control-A (Command-A). The Shift key lets you add to a selection; the Alt (Option) key lets you subtract.

INVERTING A SELECTION

Sometimes it's easier to select everything that you don't want selected and then invert the selection. I use this method all the time to select a complex subject on a simple background. Using the Magic Wand and Quick Selection tools, I can easily select the background (**Figure 6.10**) and then, using the keyboard shortcut Control-Shift-I (Command-Shift-I), invert the selection so that the subject is now the object that is selected. This allows me to do things like apply adjustments to the subject or even cut it from the background and insert a new background (**Figure 6.11**).

COPY AND PASTE

If you want to copy a selected item, use the keyboard shortcut Control-C (Command-C) to copy it to the clipboard (the temporary memory space). You can also access this command by choosing Edit > Copy. To paste the copied item into the current photo, use the keyboard shortcut Control-V (Command-V).

REFINING A SELECTION

Sometimes you will need a little help to make your selection more accurate. For this, use the Refine Edge function. Activate it by choosing Select > Refine Edge (**Figure 6.12**).

The Refine Edge dialog allows you to use viewing methods other than the marching ants to visualize the selected area. You can isolate the selection against a black or white background, or use a custom color. The Refine Edge tool includes options to smooth, feather, and contract or expand the selection edge. I usually use a 1-pixel feather to slightly blur the edge of the selection. This blends the edges better and gives good results (**Figure 6.13**).

FIGURE 6.13
The Refine Edge tool allows you to better visualize your selection and modify it as needed.

THE POWER OF ADJUSTMENT LAYERS

All of the adjustments that we have performed thus far have been applied directly to the image. There is another way to apply adjustments that is less destructive, less permanent, and very customizable. It involves something called adjustment layers, and once you start using them you may never go back to the old methods again. First, it would probably help to know what layers are.

If you think of your image as a printed picture, a layer is like laying another sheet over the top of it. It can be transparent, it can contain other images, and it could even have an effect or text on it. They can also be stacked, layer upon layer, on top of your original image. The beauty is that they can be manipulated independent of the bottom image so that you never damage your original.

On the right side of your Editor interface, you will find the Layers panel in the Full edit tab. When you have an image open, it will be listed as the Background layer in the Layers panel (**Figure 6.14**). Any new layers that you create will go on top of the Background layer and interact with it.

The adjustment layers can be found at the bottom of the Layers panel. Click the icon that looks like a half black, half white circle. This will pop up a menu of adjustments that can be applied on top of the background image; you can also find them by choosing Layer > New Adjustment Layer and then the desired effect.

FIGURE 6.14
Opening an image automatically creates the Background layer in the Layers panel.

FIGURE 6.15
To create an adjustment layer, click the black and white circle at the bottom of the Layers panel.

FIGURE 6.16
Levels adjustments for the new layer can be made in the Adjustments panel.

FIGURE 6.17
You can reduce the effect of the layer adjustment by lowering the Opacity setting of the layer.

LEVELS ADJUSTMENT LAYERS

One of the most commonly used adjustment layers is the Levels adjustment. We've already used this, but we will be able to use it in a more flexible and versatile way by applying it as a layer.

1. Click the New Adjustment Layer icon and then select Levels from the pop-up menu (**Figure 6.15**).

2. Make your Levels adjustments in the dialog that appears beneath the Layers panel (**Figure 6.16**).

3. Adjust the Opacity setting of the new layer to control how much of the effect you want on the background image. This is kind of like fading the effect (**Figure 6.17**).

You can turn the layer on and off by clicking the eyeball icon on the left side of the layer. You can also go back at any time and re-adjust the Levels adjustment by double-clicking the gear icon on the right side of the layer.

LAYER MASKS

Another feature of the adjustment layer is the layer mask. Whenever an adjustment layer is created, it comes with a mask, which is indicated by the white rectangular box on the layer. This mask is white by default, which means that it lets the entire effect of the layer be visible. If you were to change the color of the mask to black, it would conceal the entire layer effect. Here is the best part: You can paint on the white mask with a black brush to conceal part of the adjustment layer and let it affect only the part of the image that needs it. So let's say I have an image like the one in **Figure 6.18**, where I wanted the sky to be darker. To customize the mask, I would do the following:

FIGURE 6.18
This image needs to have the sky darkened a little.

1. Create a Levels adjustment layer and drag the middle gray point to the right to darken the entire image.

2. Set the foreground color to black and the background color to white by pressing the D key; these are the default colors. If the foreground color is not set to black, press the X key to switch the colors.

3. Paint on the mountains with the Brush tool to hide the adjustment. You will see the black area where the painting is occurring on the mask icon on the layer. (**Figure 6.19**) Adjust the brush size by using the bracket keys. A smaller brush is necessary for the detailed section where the mountains meet the sky.

FIGURE 6.19
The Levels adjust-
ment layer's effect
on the mountains is
concealed by paint-
ing with a black
brush on the layer
mask.

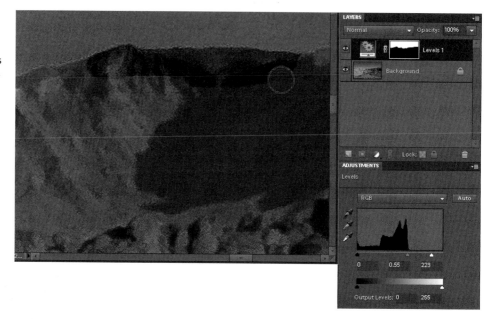

4. When done painting in all of the ground area, adjust the layer's Opacity setting to reduce the strength of the adjustment on the sky.

Figure 6.20 shows a before view on the left and an after view on the right. You can see how nicely the mask darkened the sky while concealing the adjustment from the foreground. Notice that thanks to the layer mask the mountains on the right side of the image have not been affected by the Levels adjustment.

FIGURE 6.20
The before is on the
left and the after is
on the right. Notice
that only the sky
was affected by the
Levels adjustment
layer.

USING A SELECTION IN A MASK

Remember when I said that selections would come in handy for selectively applying adjustments to images? Well, here is a perfect example. Using the brush to paint on the mask can be very time consuming and is not always accurate. This time, let's use the same image with the same adjustment. But instead of a brush, we will use the Quick Selection tool to fill in our mask.

1. Start with the same image and Levels adjustment layer as the previous exercise. Press A to activate the Quick Selection tool.

2. In the Layers panel, click the Background layer to make it the active layer (it should turn dark gray and the thumbnail of the image will have a white border around it).

3. Paint on the sky with the Quick Selection tool, adjusting the size of the brush using the bracket keys. Keep adding to the selection until the entire sky is selected (**Figure 6.21**).

FIGURE 6.21
Instead of painting on the mask, a selection is made of the sky on the background layer.

4. Press Control-Shift-I (Command-Shift-I) to invert the selection. This will make the mountains the selected part of the image.

5. Click the white rectangle in the Levels adjustment layer to make it active, making sure to click right on the white box.

6. Choose Edit > Fill Selection.

7. When the Fill Layer dialog opens, select Black from the Contents drop-down menu. Click OK (**Figure 6.22**).

8. Press Control-D (Command-D) to remove the selection, and then adjust the Opacity setting to about 75%.

FIGURE 6.22
After clicking the layer mask to make it active, the selection is filled with black.

Even though that seems like many more steps, it actually only took about 30 seconds to do. That's a lot faster than using the brush to paint on the mask and get all of the mountain edges just right.

> **NOTE**
>
> This image is included in the bonus materials, so be sure to download it and try this on your own (see Introduction). It is a PSD file and includes the Levels adjustment layer. The file name is mountains with adjustment layer.psd.

CHANGING BLEND MODES

A blend mode determines how a layer will interact with the layer or layers beneath it. The default blend mode is Normal, but there are 25 different modes to choose from. They are divided into five groups, organized by general effect (**Figure 6.23**).

- **Group 1** These modes generally have a darkening effect.

- **Group 2** These modes have a lightening effect.

- **Group 3** These modes will either lighten or darken depending on the layers, but they generally have the most effect on contrast.

- **Group 4** These modes will let you see differences between layers.

- **Group 5** These modes deal with color.

Most of the time, you will use only a few of the modes: Normal, Multiply, Screen, Overlay, Hard Light, and Soft Light. Some of these modes can be applied like an adjustment layer due to their blending properties.

FIGURE 6.23
The blend modes control how layers interact with each other.

DARKEN WITH MULTIPLY

A quick way to darken a light image is to duplicate its layer and then apply the Multiply blend mode.

1. Open your image and create a duplicate layer copy by pressing Control-J (Command-J) (**Figure 6.24**).

2. Change the blend mode to Multiply (**Figure 6.25**).

3. Adjust the Opacity setting.

LIGHTEN WITH SCREEN

If you want to achieve the opposite effect—lightening—try using the Screen blend mode.

1. Open your image and create a duplicate layer copy by pressing Control-J (Command-J) (**Figure 6.26**).

2. Change the blend mode to Screen (**Figure 6.27**).

3. Adjust the Opacity setting.

ADDING A MASK

If you like the effect you get from duplicating and changing the blend mode but it's not right for the entire image, you can always add a mask and then paint in the effect—just like we did with the Levels adjustment layer. An adjustment layer adds a mask automatically, but duplicating the background does not. Add a mask by clicking the Add Layer Mask icon in the Layers panel (**Figure 6.28**); or go to the Layer menu and select Layer Mask and choose between Reveal All (a white mask) or Hide All (a black mask). Once the mask is in place, simply paint on it with a black or white brush to conceal or reveal the effect.

FIGURE 6.24
A copy of the background is created by using the keyboard shortcut Control-J (Command-J).

FIGURE 6.25
Changing the blend mode of the top layer to Multiply makes the image darker.

FIGURE 6.26
A copy of the background is created by using the keyboard shortcut Control-J (Command-J).

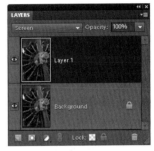

FIGURE 6.27
Changing the blend mode of the top layer to Screen makes the image brighter.

FIGURE 6.28
You can add a layer mask to the active layer by clicking the Add Layer Mask icon.

MAKING MASKS FROM SELECTIONS

You can also use a selection to create a mask.

1. Open your image and then duplicate the background by pressing Control-J (Command-J) (**Figure 6.29**).

2. Grab the Quick Selection tool from the toolbar and paint a selection onto the area where you want the layer effect to be visible (**Figure 6.30**).

3. Click the Add Layer Mask icon at the bottom of the Layers panel (notice that the selected area is white on the mask icon; the unselected area is black) (**Figure 6.31**).

4. Change the blend mode to Screen.

5. If the effect is not strong enough, press Control-J (Command-J) to duplicate the layer copy, which multiplies the effect. If it's too strong, lower the opacity of the top layer (**Figure 6.32**).

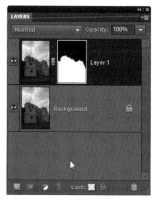

FIGURE 6.31
Clicking the Add Layer Mask icon with a selection active automatically creates a mask.

FIGURE 6.29
Duplicate the background layer by pressing Control-J (Command-J).

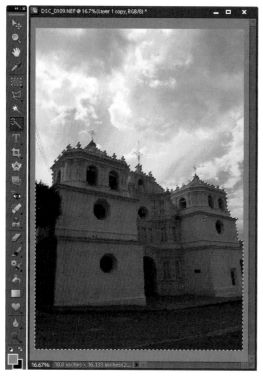

FIGURE 6.30
The Quick Selection tool is used to select the buildings and foreground.

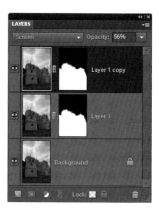

FIGURE 6.32
The Screen blend mode is applied and then the layer is duplicated to intensify the effect.

Chapter 6 Assignments

We really started to cover some ground in Chapter 6, and these tools will take some practice before you feel comfortable using them. That's why we have these lessons. Everything we do builds a foundation for better and faster editing down the road. Let's take a little practice time with these specialized tools before moving on.

Heal and Clone

I'm sure it won't be too hard to find a few images that have little spots that need healing. Maybe you want to get rid of that freckle that's been bugging you all these years. No problem. Just open the image, grab the Healing Brush tool, and start clicking. Try painting with small strokes for things like stray hairs. Then give the Clone Stamp tool a try. Just remember to hold the Alt (Option) key and click a source before trying to clone.

Make Selections

Using the selection tools can be a challenge, so spend a little time with each one. Use the Rectangular and Elliptical Marquee tools, and don't forget to hold the Shift and Alt (Option) keys to add and subtract. Then move on to the Lasso tools. Take an image with a well-defined subject and then use the tools to select it. Then give the Quick Selection tool a try and see how easy it is to make complex selections.

Add an Adjustment Layer

We only covered the Levels adjustment layer in this chapter, but there are others you can play with as well, like the Brightness/Contrast layer or the Photo Filter layer (a favorite of mine for warming an image). Open a photo and give each of them a try. If you don't like the effect, simply drag the layer to the trash can icon at the bottom of the Layers panel. Try using more than one adjustment and then playing with the Opacity setting to see how it fades the effect.

Paint on a Mask

The easiest way to learn about masks is to just dive in, so here is what I want you to do. Open an image and apply a Levels adjustment layer. Move the gray triangle pretty far to the right to make the image dark. Press the D key for the default colors. If black is not set to the foreground, press the X key. Now grab your brush by pressing the B key and start painting on the image. You should see the darkness of the adjustment layer disappear wherever you paint. You can also paint with gray to reduce the concealing effect of the brush. Just go to the brush options at the top of the image panel and set the Opacity to something lower than 100%. Try 75%, then 50%, and then 25%. You can get much more subtle results this way.

Share your results with the book's Flickr group!

Join the group here: flickr.com/groups/elements_fromsnapshotstogreatshots

7

ISO 200
1/1000 sec.
f/2.8
70mm lens

Making Your Images Pop!

FINE-TUNING AND SPECIAL EFFECTS

Now that we have a good foundation of image editing skills, it's time to start taking things up a notch. Here's the thing: Most great-looking images are treated with basic image-processing steps like the ones we have covered. But a good editor can move beyond the basics and add little effects to the image that really make it stand out. It doesn't have to be anything over the top either. Sometimes it's a subtle thing like a gradient added to a sky, or maybe a vignette to add emphasis and focus to a subject. This chapter will cover effects and treatments that I use daily to add some pop to my pictures.

A concrete texture layer
added a little grunge.

I love this old ruin that I found while exploring the Angkor region of
Cambodia. It reminds me of the kind of ancient structure one might find
in Rome. Unfortunately, the light I had to work with was less than great.
But sometimes these are the best images for applying special effects—
like this textured grunge layer, which makes the photo look old.

The edges of the image were darkened with a vignette effect.

A sepia adjustment was added to make the image look older.

A Levels adjustment layer added some needed contrast.

ISO 200
1/60 sec.
f/9
24mm lens

SHARPENING WITH HIGH PASS

I'm not really sure what the purpose of the High Pass filter is, but I do know that it is most often used for some crazy sharpening. Since we just covered layers, this is a great place to start, because we need a layer copy of the background to make this work.

1. Open your image and then duplicate the background layer by pressing Control-J (Command-J).

2. With the layer copy selected in the Layers panel, choose Filter > Other > High Pass.

3. A dialog opens with a gray-looking conversion of the image. Take the Radius slider to zero and then move it to the right until the edges start showing up. How high you go depends on the resolution of the image and the degree of sharpness you want. Click the OK button when you are done (**Figure 7.1**).

4. In the Layers panel, change the blend mode to Soft Light (**Figure 7.2**).

Changing the blend mode to Overlay and Hard Light will intensify the sharpening effect. To make things look more grungy, you can try re-processing the High Pass filter with a higher setting. If you like the effect but want a little more, duplicate the High Pass layer copy to multiply the effect. And remember that if you don't like it, you can just drag the layer copy to the Trash and start over. It's all about experimentation.

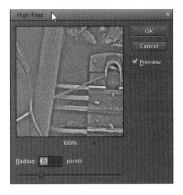

FIGURE 7.1
The High Pass filter settings.

FIGURE 7.2
Changing the blend mode of the High Pass layer.

THE WILD BLUE YONDER

Getting really blue skies is not always easy when you are out in the field. You are at the mercy of the weather and atmospheric conditions, and sometimes the best-looking skies don't turn out the way you remember them. Usually the problem is that they are too light and not very colorful. Here are a couple of techniques that will bring them back to life.

DARKENING BLUE SKIES

This method is similar to one that we used in the last chapter. It involves just a couple of steps, but it can dramatically improve the look of your skies.

1. Open your image, grab the Quick Selection tool, and select your sky (**Figure 7.3**).

FIGURE 7.3
Select the sky with the Quick Selection tool.

2. Click the New Adjustment Layer icon and select Levels (**Figure 7.4**).

3. When the Adjustments panel opens, move the gray triangle to the right to darken the skies; slide the white triangle to the left to increase contrast and brighten any clouds (**Figure 7.5**).

FIGURE 7.4
Adding a Levels adjustment layer.

FIGURE 7.5
Adjust the Levels settings to darken the sky.

4. If the image needs to be darker, move the black triangle to the right.

Using a Levels adjustment layer also has the added benefit of adding some saturation as part of the darkening process.

PRESERVING AND FLATTENING LAYERS

We have created a lot of layers in the last two chapters, but what exactly should you do with them when you are done? Well, it all depends on whether you want to come back and work with them later. You should know that layers increase the size of your image file. Depending on the number and type of layers, you could double or even triple the file size. If you don't think you will need to use the layers again, you can do something called *flattening*, which moves all of the layers to the background layer. And most file formats, such as JPEG, do not support saving layers, so the simple act of saving your image as a JPEG will flatten it. To manually flatten layers, choose Layer › Flatten Image.

To preserve your layers for editing down the road, save your file as a PSD or TIFF file. These file formats support layers and will keep them safe for the next time you open your image. Just be sure to select the Save Layers check box in the Save As dialog.

USING A GRADIENT ON SKIES

When shooting landscapes, I like to use a gradient filter that darkens the top of the sky and gets gradually lighter toward the ground. I don't always have one with me, but I know I can easily take care of it in Elements.

1. Open a photo and apply your standard processing.

2. Press the D key to set black as your default foreground color.

3. Click the New Adjustment Layer icon and select Gradient (**Figure 7.6**).

4. When the Gradient options open, select the black to transparent gradient from the Gradient drop-down menu (**Figure 7.7**).

FIGURE 7.6
Apply a gradient by clicking the New Adjustment Layer icon.

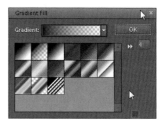

FIGURE 7.7
Select the black to transparent gradient.

5. Select Linear from the Style drop-down menu, and change the Angle setting to –90° (**Figure 7.8**).

6. Finally, change the blend mode to Soft Light. To intensify the effect, duplicate the adjustment layer by pressing Control-J (Command-J) (**Figure 7.9**).

CREATING BLACK AND WHITE IMAGES

There's something timeless and classic about great black and white photos. When done well, they conjure up visions of Ansel Adams or Edward Weston. But you don't have to struggle with chemicals and enlargers to create your own classic shots, because you are using Adobe Photoshop Elements. In fact, making a black and white image is so simple, you can do it with just a couple of clicks. The other benefit of creating a black and white is that you can sometimes turn a not-so-great photo into a work of art.

Figure 7.10 had some potential when it was taken, but the flat light turned it into something less than spectacular. That doesn't mean it's a complete loss. All it takes is a quick run through the black and white conversion utility to make it look much better.

FIGURE 7.8
Change the gradient's Angle setting to –90°.

FIGURE 7.9
Duplicate the layer to intensify the effect.

FIGURE 7.10
The landscape photo prior to black and white conversion.

1. Open the file and perform standard image processing, but don't worry about the color.

2. Choose Enhance > Convert to Black and White (**Figure 7.11**).

3. Select one of the Style presets and then adjust the Red, Green, Blue, and Contrast sliders to fine-tune the effect. Click OK to apply (**Figure 7.12**).

You could go with the default conversion, but to really take it to the next level, do the following:

1. Duplicate the background by pressing Control-J (Command-J).

2. Choose Filter > Other > High Pass.

3. Adjust the setting to get more edge detail and sharpness (**Figure 7.13**), click OK, and set the blend mode to Soft Light.

4. Click the New Adjustment Layer icon, select Levels, and fine-tune the look of the image (**Figure 7.14**).

FIGURE 7.11
Convert to Black and White is in the Enhance menu.

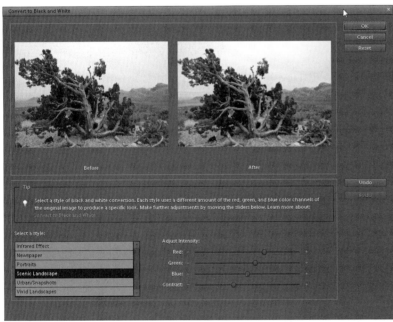

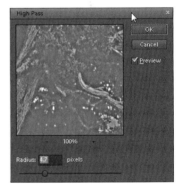

FIGURE 7.13
Add a High Pass filter layer to increase sharpness.

FIGURE 7.12
Select a Style preset to change the look of the black and white effect.

FIGURE 7.14
Finish off the
effect with a Levels
adjustment layer.

GOING WIDE WITH A PANORAMA

Panoramic images have gained in popularity over the past few years. Part of the reason is that it is now easier than ever to make one, thanks to advances in pano-making software like Elements.

Making a great pano starts with the photos. When you take pano shots, make sure that you hold the camera level and overlap your pictures by 20–30 percent.

1. Select your images in the Organizer and choose File > New > Photomerge Panorama (**Figure 7.15**). If you shot raw files, they will open first in Camera Raw; otherwise, they will open directly in the Editor.

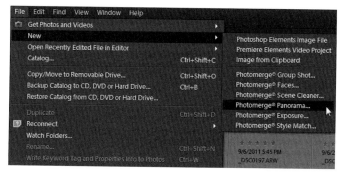

FIGURE 7.15
Access the Photo-
merge Panorama
option by clicking
New in the File
menu.

2. In the Photomerge dialog, click Add Open Files. Make sure the Layout setting is Auto, and select the Vignette Removal check box. Click OK to begin the merging process (**Figure 7.16**).

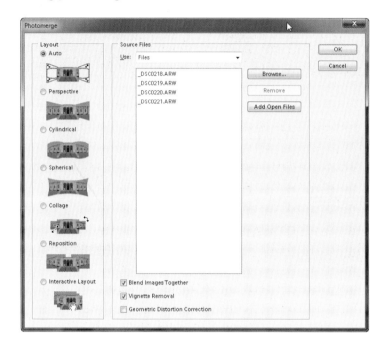

3. When the pano is done, a box will pop up asking if you want to fill in the edges. Click Yes to have the checkered areas filled in automatically (**Figure 7.17**).

4. To complete the pano, go to the Layer menu and click Flatten Image (**Figure 7.18**).

FIGURE 7.17
Clean Edges will fill in the missing pieces of your assembled panorama.

FIGURE 7.18
Flatten the layers to complete the pano.

5. Crop the edges off your image, if necessary, and then enjoy (**Figure 7.19**).

FIGURE 7.19
The completed panorama, made from four images.

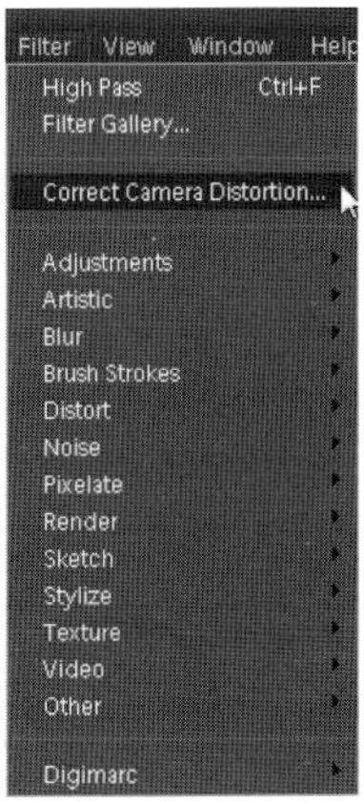

ADDING EMPHASIS WITH A VIGNETTE

Adding a vignette to an image has become pretty popular lately because it's a great way to key in on a subject and draw your eyes into the frame. There are a couple of ways to add a vignette, and each one has its own merits.

The first method uses the camera distortion correction utility. Some lenses actually add some vignetting that you might want to remove with this utility, but we are going to use it to add a vignette.

1. Open the file and choose Filter > Correct Camera Distortion (**Figure 7.20**).

2. When the dialog opens, drag the Amount slider to the left to apply the vignette. Then use the Midpoint slider to adjust how far into the image the vignette goes (**Figure 7.21**).

3. Click the OK button to apply the vignette.

FIGURE 7.20
Access the Correct Camera Distortion function in the Filter menu.

FIGURE 7.21
Drag the Amount slider to the left to increase the vignette.

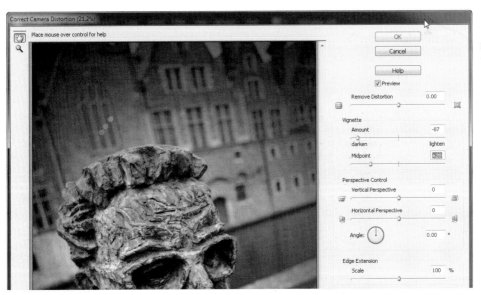

This method works pretty well, but there is little control over how dark the vignette is. If you want a little more control, try the following:

1. Open the image and then click the New Layer icon at the bottom of the Layers panel to add a blank layer on top of the background (**Figure 7.22**).

2. Use the Rectangular Marquee tool to draw a loose selection around your subject (**Figure 7.23**).

3. Press Control-Alt-D (Command-Option-D) to open the Feather Selection option. Set it to a high number, like 250 pixels (**Figure 7.24**).

4. Press Control-Shift-I (Command-Shift-I) to invert your selection, and press Alt-Backspace (Option-Delete) to fill the selection with black.

5. Change the blend mode to Multiply, and lower the Opacity setting to something that works for your photo (**Figure 7.25**).

6. Press Control-D (Command-D) to remove the selection.

FIGURE 7.22
Create a new blank layer by clicking the New Layer icon.

FIGURE 7.23
Draw a selection around your subject.

FIGURE 7.24
Feather the selection to soften the edges.

FIGURE 7.25
Fill the layer and change the blend mode to Multiply.

GETTING A NEW PERSPECTIVE

Have you ever taken a photograph of a building with a wide angle lens? Were you surprised to find that it was totally distorted when you saw it on your computer? You know what I mean; all those lines that looked so straight and vertical are now angled toward the middle of the photograph (**Figure 7.26**). It's called lens distortion, and it has more to do with the angle that your camera was at when you took the photograph than the wideness of the lens, although there is distortion there too. You could correct this problem by using a special tilt-shift lens that is used by architectural photographers, but it would cost you about $2000. Instead, let's let the Elements Editor have a crack at it.

FIGURE 7.26
A wide angle lens can make buildings appear to lean in toward the center of the frame.

1. Open your image in the Editor and then choose Filter > Correct Camera Distortion (**Figure 7.27**).

2. When the Correct Camera Distortion dialog opens, make sure the Show Grid check box is selected. This will put an alignment grid on top of your image and make it easier to get your lines parallel.

3. Drag the Vertical Perspective slider to the left. Keep dragging until all the vertical lines are parallel (**Figure 7.28**).

FIGURE 7.27
Use the Correct Camera Distortion function for fixing perspective problems.

FIGURE 7.28
Use the Vertical
Perspective slider
to correct for lean-
ing buildings.

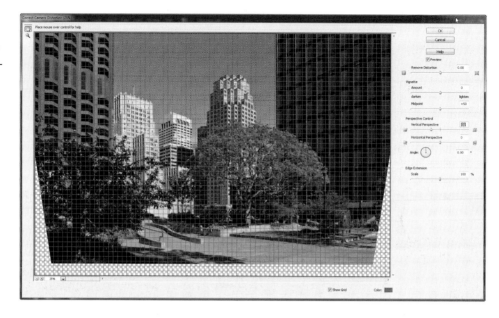

4. You will notice that part of the image is now angled and transparent. To fix it, move the Edge Extension slider a little to the right to expand the image and make the cut-off areas disappear. Click OK to return to the Editor (**Figure 7.29**).

FIGURE 7.29
Use the Edge
Extension slider or
just crop the image
to finish.

CREATING GRUNGE WITH A TEXTURE LAYER

This final effect uses a texture image to create a grunge effect on your photo. It is very popular and can add new dimension to your image. I am using a texture image of concrete, but you can use whatever you like. In fact, the next time you are out walking around with your camera, take some photos of things like concrete, wood, stone, and so on, and build your own catalog of textures.

1. Open the image that you want to grunge up, along with your texture photo (**Figure 7.30**).

FIGURE 7.30
Open a textured photo to copy and paste it as a new layer in your image.

2. Click the texture image to make it active, and then press Control-A (Command-A) to select the entire image.

3. Click your other photo, and then press Control-V (Command-V) to paste in the texture image.

4. Press Control-T (Command-T) to activate the Free Transform tool to resize the texture layer. Grab the corners and stretch them out until it covers the entire photo. Press Enter when you're done (**Figure 7.31**).

FIGURE 7.31
Use the Free Transform tool to resize the texture layer to fit the image.

5. Change the blend mode of the texture layer to Overlay, and then lower the opacity.

Try combining this effect with some of the others that we have learned in this chapter, such as a vignette, a Levels adjustment layer, or maybe even a sepia-colored Photo Filter adjustment layer. The only limit is your imagination (**Figure 7.32**).

FIGURE 7.32
Add other adjustment layers to create new effects.

Chapter 7 Assignments

The great thing about the effects in this chapter is that they can be combined to create completely different looks for your photo. They can also be applied to specific areas through the use of masks. The best thing to do with all these effects is to play with them, see how they work, and discover the possibilities that they present.

Blue Sky with a Gradient

The power of layers is in their ability to be stacked up. Find one of your photos with a blue sky, and use a Levels adjustment layer to make it darker. Then add a gradient to darken the top of the photo. Play with the different blend modes to see how they change the look of the layer, and then use the Opacity slider to fade the effect.

From Soft to Razor Sharp

The High Pass filter can add subtle sharpening, or it can be very heavy and grungy looking, depending on the radius you select. Create a copy of your Background layer and then use the High Pass filter with a small radius, like 3. Then delete that layer and try it again with a High Pass setting of 10. Experiment with the blend modes, switching between Soft Light, Overlay, and Hard Light.

Create a Black and White from Color

The example used in this chapter for creating a black and white was a landscape shot, but you aren't limited to trees and mountains. Lots of subjects look great in black and white. Open up some people shots and try the different black and white styles.

Shoot Panoramas

If you don't have any photos that are ready for making panos, why not grab your camera and shoot a few? Remember to overlap your photos by 20–30 percent. Also, don't use a lens that is too wide, or Photomerge will have a tough time dealing with the lens distortion. Panorama file sizes can get quite large, so if you have a high-megapixel camera, try shooting in JPEG mode and selecting a smaller image size; most cameras will let you choose large, medium, or small JPEGs. Start with two overlapping images, and then try some wide three- and four-image panos.

Share your results with the book's Flickr group!

Join the group here: flickr.com/groups/elements_fromsnapshotstogreatshots

8

ISO 200
1/200 sec.
f/5.6
102mm lens

After the Edits

TIME TO DO SOMETHING WITH THAT GREAT-LOOKING PHOTO

We have edited and organized—but what fun is it to take pictures and then just squirrel them away on your hard drive? You have worked hard to improve your image editing skills, and this chapter is all about showing them off. One of the wonderful things about the digital medium is that there are so many options for showing off your work, whether you decide to make prints, create an online gallery, or just send some photos in an email. Let's take a look at a few of the many options that Elements offers.

PORING OVER THE PICTURE

The Recovery slider helped bring back definition in the clouds.

I used a High Pass sharpening effect to get more detail in the rock.

ISO 400
1/125 sec.
f/9
11mm lens

I have been to Nevada more times than I can count, and I spent most of that time in Las Vegas. I'm not much of a gambler, so instead I spent my free time roaming the desert in search of a great landscape shot. But never in all my trips had I visited Valley of Fire State Park. So when I got the invitation from a friend this past September, I jumped at the chance. I can say with some certainty that it will not be my last visit.

I warmed the white balance considerably to add more color to the sandstone.

A Levels adjustment layer darkened the lower portion of the image.

MAKING GREAT-LOOKING PRINTS

You might think that making a print from your photo would be a straightforward operation, and it is for the most part. There are a few settings you should tweak, though, to get the best possible quality from every print.

> **NOTE**
>
> I use Epson inkjet printers for my home printing, but you will probably have similar settings for your HP, Canon, Brother, or other inkjet printer. Consult your printer's manual for specific instructions.

SHARPENING FOR PRINTS

We covered this in a previous chapter, but it's worth repeating: Sharpening for a print is different than sharpening for onscreen use. You will need to apply more sharpening than you think is necessary when you are going to be making an inkjet print. The reason is that when a print is made, the ink that is laid out on the photo paper has a tendency to spread slightly as it soaks into the paper fibers. There can also be a difference in the paper material in relation to the amount of sharpening needed. Glossy papers tend to hold the ink together well, so less sharpening is needed. Matte or fiber papers allow the ink to spread more and will require more sharpening. You will need to do a little testing to see how much sharpening you can get away with when making your own prints.

SETTING UP THE PRINTER

The Print window looks the same whether it is launched from the Organizer or the Editor. One advantage to printing from the Organizer is that it is easier to select multiple images for printing. Just select the photos you want to print, and then choose File > Print or press Control-P (Command-P) to launch the Print dialog.

If you have multiple images open in the Editor, you can send them all to the Print window by Control-clicking (Command-clicking) each one in the Project Bin first.

The Print window has several parts, with different options depending on your desired results (**Figure 8.1**). The left side shows thumbnails of the selected images. The center section is a preview of what the print will look like. The right section is a numbered list of options to follow when preparing to make a print.

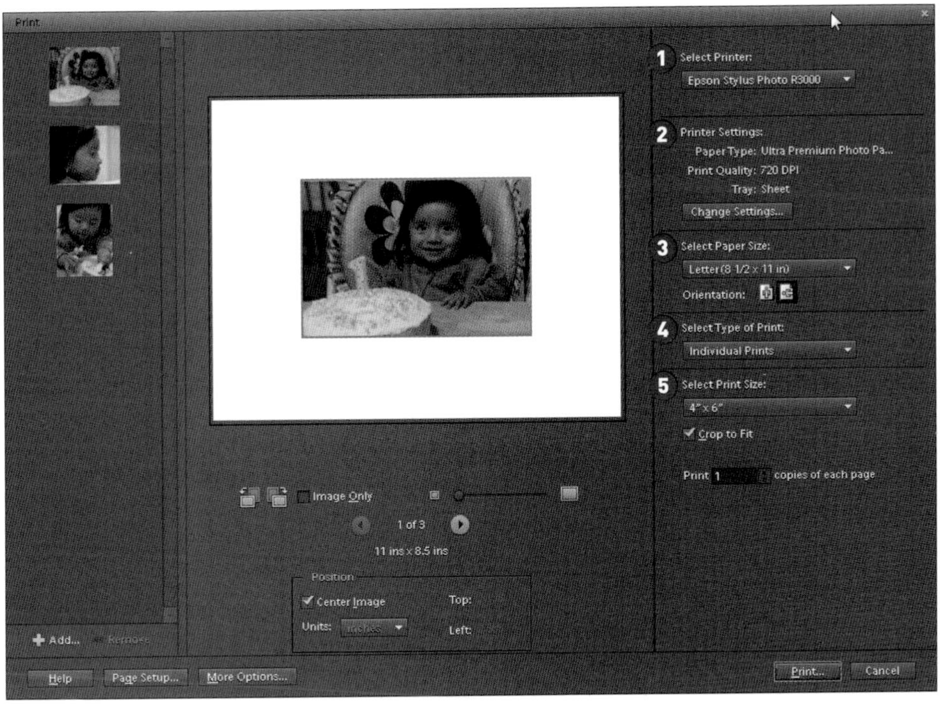

FIGURE 8.1
The Print window.

1. This drop-down list contains all the printers installed on your computer. Select the appropriate one.

2. This is where you will change print settings such as Paper Type and Print Quality.

3. You can select your paper size from a wide variety of choices in this drop-down list. This is specifically for the size of the paper, not the size of the print. You can define custom paper sizes if yours is not in the list.

4. If there are multiple images loaded in the Print window, you need to decide if you want individual prints or a package, where you can fit multiple images on one printed sheet.

5. The final option determines the size of the print, along with sizing constraints and the number of copies.

Most of these are pretty straightforward, but there are a couple of other choices worth mentioning that will make your prints look better.

FIGURE 8.2
Select the proper paper type.

CHANGE SETTINGS TO IMPROVE QUALITY

In section 2, click the Change Settings button and select the proper paper from the Paper Type drop-down menu (**Figure 8.2**). Each paper type prints differently, and your printer will make adjustments depending on what you select. Also, I recommend using photo papers made by your printer manufacturer. They are specifically engineered to work with your printer and will most often deliver superior results.

Beneath the paper type is the Print Quality setting. Depending on the printer, pressing this might send you to the printer setup window. To improve the quality of your printed images, be sure to change this option to a higher setting. On an Epson printer such as the one I use, the setting should be changed from Speed to Quality.

PRINTING ON A MAC

If you are a Mac user, you might notice some small differences in the printer interface from those shown here. That's because printing functions are mainly handled by the operating system and not Elements. The settings recommended in this section should be available for your printer but may be accessed in a different location. Please consult your owner's manual for instructions on changing image quality and color management.

COLOR MANAGEMENT

An important part of getting good-looking prints is having effective color management. This is the process your computer and printer use to determine what colors should look like in your prints. Click the More Options button at the bottom of the Print window and then select Color Management from the list on the left side of the More Options dialog (**Figure 8.3**).

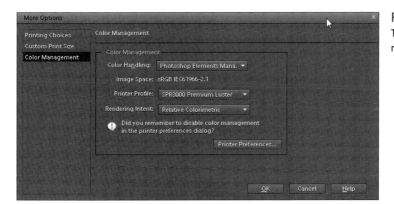

FIGURE 8.3
The Color Management options.

Select Photoshop Elements Manages Color from the Color Handling drop-down menu. Then change the Printer Profile setting to match the paper you are using. This list should have been installed when you installed your printer and more than likely contains paper profiles for papers that are made by your printer manufacturer. If you don't have any paper profiles, select Adobe RGB. Leave the Rendering Intent setting at Relative Colorimetric.

Click the Printer Preferences button. This will open up a preferences panel that is specific to your printer. Look for an option that turns off any printer color management. You need to do this because we have already told Elements that we want it to handle color management duties. If you are using an Epson printer, look for the Mode setting and set it to Off (No Color Adjustment) (**Figure 8.4**). Click the OK button. With all of the preferences set, you can now click the Print button in the Print window to make your first print.

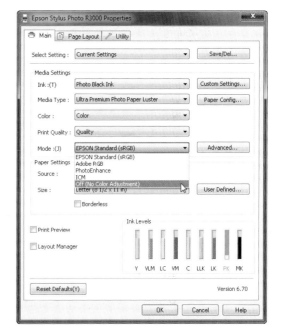

FIGURE 8.4
Turn off the printer's color management.

CREATING A GALLERY-STYLE PRINT

One of the ways I enhance the look of my prints is to give them the appearance that they are from a gallery. This means they look like they have a wide, white mat around them, along with some text below, as seen in **Figure 8.5**. This is easy to do and makes your prints look fantastic.

FIGURE 8.5
A gallery print
ready for hanging.

1. Open the image in the Editor and then press Control-N (Command-N) to create a new document. Select the size of the print you want to make (**Figure 8.6**).

2. When the new document opens, click back on your photograph, press Control-A (Command-A) to select all, click back on the new document, and press Control-V (Command-V) to paste the picture into the blank page.

FIGURE 8.6
Create a new blank document.

3. The photo layer should be active, so press Control-T (Command-T) to activate the Free Transform tool and then resize the image to give a good border around the edges. Press the Enter key (**Figure 8.7**).

FIGURE 8.7
Use the Free Transform tool to resize the photo layer.

4. Press the V key to activate the Move tool and then position the photo on the blank page, leaving substantially more space at the bottom than on the top and sides (**Figure 8.8**).

FIGURE 8.8
Use the Move tool to reposition the photo.

5. Press the T key to activate the Text tool. In the option bar above the image window, pick your font, set the justification to Centered, select a font size, and pick black as your font color (**Figure 8.9**).

6. Click the white border with the Text tool and type out something fitting for your image. Drag over the text to select it, and use the Font Size option to adjust the size of the font. Click the check mark on the option bar when you are happy with your text (it appears on the bar after you type something on the image).

7. In the Layers panel, lower the Opacity setting of the text layer to about 25% to finish off the effect (**Figure 8.10**).

PRINTING A CONTACT SHEET

The term *contact sheet* dates back to the days of film and darkrooms, when a photographer would lay the negatives on a piece of photo paper. The negatives would then be exposed to light while in contact with the paper, making one large print containing a bunch of small positive images. This was an economical way of looking at the photos and deciding which ones to enlarge. Now you have the luxury of looking at all of your images as thumbnails on your computer screen instead of printing them. There may, however, be instances where you want to print a large sheet of thumbnails to deliver to a client or friend. And once again, Elements makes this extremely easy to do.

FIGURE 8.10
Lower the opacity of the text layer.

1. In the Organizer, select the photos that you want included in your contact sheet.

2. Click the Create tab and select Photo Prints.

3. Click Print Contact Sheet (**Figure 8.11**).

4. The Print window will open, looking very similar to the last time we opened it but with a few different options. In section 4, deselect the Crop to Fit check box to see the entire image, not a cropped version. Then select the number of columns that you want on each page (**Figure 8.12**).

FIGURE 8.11
The Photo Prints options.

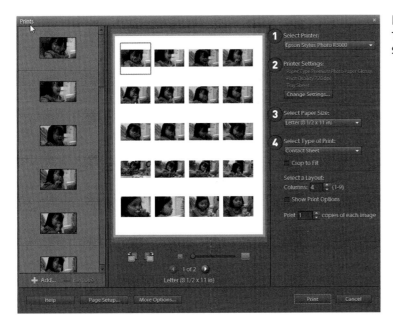

FIGURE 8.12
The Print Contact
Sheet options.

5. Click the Print button to begin the printing process.

All the options that we selected earlier in the chapter with respect to paper type, size, and color management apply here, so just refer to that section to set those up.

DEFAULT PRINTER SETTINGS IN WINDOWS

If you get tired of having to change your printer settings, you can change the defaults so that if you always print with specific paper and quality options they will be set automatically. In Windows, click Start and then Devices and Printers. Right-click on your printer and choose Printing Preferences from the menu. When the preference window opens, set up your printer as if you were going to make a print and then click OK. Now when you go to the Print window in Elements, those settings will be automatically applied.

PRINTING A PICTURE PACKAGE

Remember those photo packages that you used to get from school? You remember, the ones with a 5x7, a couple of 3x5 prints, and maybe some wallet-size prints. Well, now you can create your own picture packages so Grandma doesn't have to wait for her copies.

1. In the Organizer, select the image to print and then choose Create > Photo Prints > Print Picture Package.

2. In section 5 of the Print window, select the layout for your prints.

3. To print multiple pictures of a single image, select the Fill Page With First Photo check box.

4. Set the rest of the printer and paper options and then click the Print button (**Figure 8.13**).

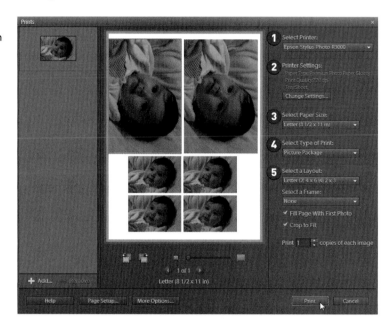

FIGURE 8.13
Package printing in Elements.

ORDERING FROM AN ONLINE PRINTER

Not everyone has a great photo printer at home, but that doesn't mean you should be without great-looking prints to hang on your wall or refrigerator. There are two online printing services available for you to use, Shutterfly and Kodak Gallery. They offer a wide variety of photo printing services, from simple 4x6 prints to great wall-hanging sizes like 20x30.

To order from one of the two services, highlight the image or images that you want to have printed and then choose Create > Photo Prints > Order Prints from... (pick one of the services). You will have to register with your name, an email address, and a password, and then you will enter the print ordering section. It's straightforward from there. Follow the prompts to choose the products that you want (**Figure 8.14**).

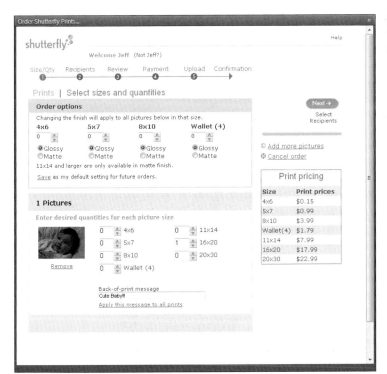

FIGURE 8.14
The Shutterfly
order screen.

A word of advice though for those of you who are shooting raw images: Do all of your corrections and then save the images as JPEGs. The raw images in the Organizer do not have any corrections applied to them even if you worked on them in Camera Raw. If you send them to the service in the raw format, you will see the unedited version in the ordering window.

PRINTING AT A LOCAL RETAILER

I have a lot of friends who love to use a retailer for their prints. These stores make it easy for you to get good-looking prints at great prices. Many of them allow you to upload your images online and then pick them up at your local store. You can also drop off a CD-ROM of photos for printing. If this is how you like to work, my advice is that you export your edited photos as JPEGs to a folder on your computer where you can either transmit them or write them to a CD. There's an easy way to do this right inside the Organizer.

1. In the Organizer, select the photos that you want to print.

2. Choose File > Export as New File(s) (**Figure 8.15**).

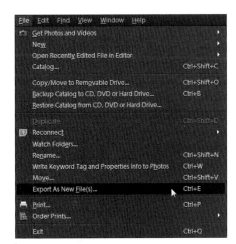

FIGURE 8.15
Using the Export as New File(s) option.

3. In the Export New Files dialog, set the File Type to JPEG, the Photo Size to Original, and the Quality to 8 or higher. In the Location section, choose a folder for the files to be saved to (**Figure 8.16**).

4. Click the Export button to begin the process.

SHARING YOUR IMAGES ONLINE

Social media sites have really exploded in the past few years. One of the reasons they are so popular is that they give everyone a chance to share their photos. There are billions of photographs being shared through sites like Facebook and Flickr, in online photo galleries like SmugMug, and at hundreds of other Web locations. So how can you get your images out there for sharing with family, friends, or the world? Well, Elements makes it pretty easy.

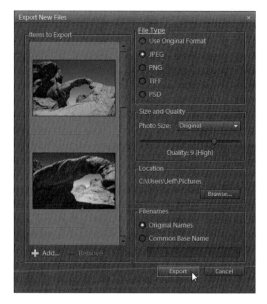

FIGURE 8.16
The Export New Files dialog.

SHARING ON FLICKR

One of the largest photo sharing sites is Flickr (**Figure 8.17**). They have been around for a long time, and it's totally free to set up an account. If you already have an account, you will need to authorize Elements to use it, which is a straightforward process.

Select photos to upload, click the Share tab, and select Share to Flickr. If you don't have an account yet, sign up at flickr.com.

Once you have authorized the account (**Figure 8.18**), Elements will open a window where you can enter all the necessary info for each image, such as tags, photosets, and who has access to see your photos (**Figure 8.19**).

Click Upload when you are done. Elements will prepare your files for online use and then upload them to your account.

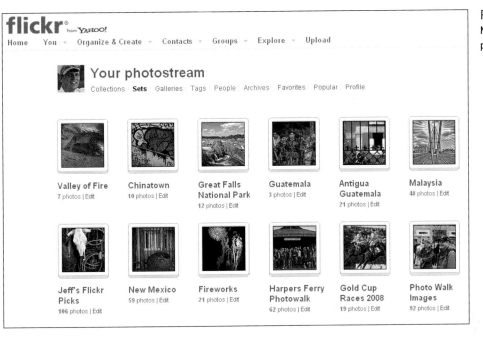

FIGURE 8.17
My personal Flickr page.

FIGURE 8.18
The Flickr authorization screen.

FIGURE 8.19
The Flickr upload window.

SHARING ON FACEBOOK

Facebook is the king of all social media sites (at least for today). It's also one of the most popular ways of sharing information and photos with friends and family. Thanks to the auto-uploading feature in Elements, sharing your images with your Facebook friends has never been easier.

Just as with Flickr, when you select photos, click the Share tab, and select Share to Facebook, you will see an authorization screen (**Figure 8.20**). When you authorize, you will be taken to your Facebook account, where you will complete the authorization (**Figure 8.21**).

The upload window will open, and you can set options like album names and who is authorized to see the photos (**Figure 8.22**).

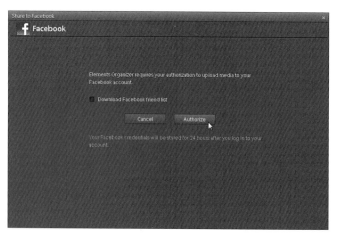

FIGURE 8.20
The Facebook authorization screen.

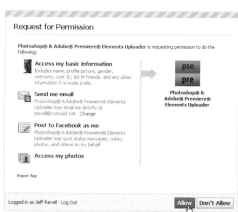

FIGURE 8.21
Permission must be granted on your Facebook page.

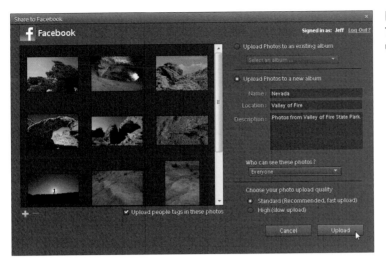

FIGURE 8.22
The Facebook
upload window.

EMAILING PHOTOS

There are two email methods for you to choose from in the Share tab. The first is called Photo Mail. It uses your photos to create an HTML email that looks more like a Web page than a standard email message. Although it is interesting to play with, I find it too long and cumbersome a process. You have to create the email using stationery presets that can be customized, and it is a fairly involved process (**Figure 8.23**).

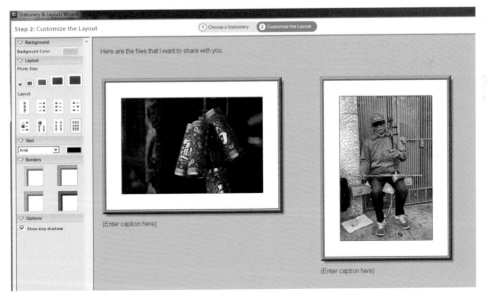

FIGURE 8.23
The Photo Mail
options.

6 Items

✔ Convert Photos to JPEGs

Maximum Photo Size:

Medium (800 x 600 px)

Quality:

9 - High

Estimated Size:

~680.00 KB, 3.90 min @ 56Kbps

FIGURE 8.24
The Email Attachments options.

When I email photos, I like to pick the images, resize them appropriately, and then save them so that I can add them to my email as attachments. That's why I prefer the Email Attachments option in the Share tab.

It's as easy as selecting the photos, clicking the Email Attachments button, and setting the options. For email, I always convert photos to JPEGs. I resize them to Medium (800x600 px), and I set the Quality to 9. This makes the photos large enough to be seen well by the recipient but not too large that they will take a long time to send or receive (**Figure 8.24**).

You will need to select a recipient for your emails. You can import your contact list or enter new contacts by clicking the contact icon above the Recipients window.

The other bit of housekeeping you will need to do before sending email from Elements is to select your email client in the preferences. In the Organizer, choose Edit > Preferences > Sharing. Then select your email client in the Email Settings section and click the OK button.

On a Mac, locate Preferences in the Adobe Elements 10 Organizer menu and then select Sharing from the sidebar options.

Chapter 8 Assignments

All right, time to put all that practice to some good and start doing something with those photographs. There are so many options available for sharing your new works of art that the only problem you might have is deciding what to do first.

Make a Big Print

This probably isn't something you will do at home, but I highly encourage you to take one of your favorite images and have it blown up big. I'm talking 16x20 or larger. Print prices today are incredibly cheap, and you really won't be able to appreciate what you have done until you have an image enlarged. So go ahead, use an online service or take a digital copy to a retailer and then GO BIG!

Set Up a Flickr Account

I have had my Flickr account for years, and it's still one of the best ways I know to share photos with family and friends. If you haven't already, take a few minutes to jump on over and set one up. It's totally free, although there is a paid option if you want a ton of storage. Also, you will need an account so that you can share your images in the Flickr group created just for this book. It's a chance for you to show off your Elements mastery to others and see what they are doing as well.

Export Your Photos to a Folder

At some point, you will want to give someone a large batch of your photos. Maybe you were the official photographer at a function, or you want to hand off a big group of family photos from your collection to a family member. Well, go ahead and use the Export function to prepare a group for sharing. Convert them to JPEG and stick them in a folder on your desktop. It's a great little trick that you are sure to use down the road. You can always delete them after you practice exporting.

Share your results with the book's Flickr group!

Join the group here: flickr.com/groups/elements_fromsnapshotstogreatshots

9

ISO 400
1/125 sec.
f/9
24mm lens

Fixing Photos

A STEP-BY-STEP LOOK AT MY EDITING WORKFLOW

Now you should have all the necessary skills to start turning your snapshots into great shots (sorry, I couldn't resist). But you still might be a little fuzzy on how all of this comes together in a workflow. In this chapter, I will take some of my images and run through the complete editing steps to make them look better. But it's not just about making them look better, it's about finishing off my creative vision for the shot, which starts the moment I put the camera to my eye and click the shutter.

I don't want this to be just a show and tell chapter. I really want you to be engaged, so every image that I am working on is available for you as part of the bonus content (register and download at peachpit.com/elements_snapshots). There is a mix of JPEG and raw images, and we will get an opportunity to do some different processing techniques to each of them. Let's go ahead and get started.

PORING OVER THE PICTURE

An adjustment layer was added to increase contrast and darken the sky.

The horizon was straightened out using the Straighten tool in Camera Raw.

ISO 100
1/80 sec.
f/4.2
35mm lens

The Recovery slider helped pull some detail back into the brightest parts of the sky.

I brightened the shadows with the Fill Light slider.

There's a debate about how much processing should be done to landscape photographs. Some people believe that you should treat them like documentary images, never to be changed, enhanced, or adjusted. Others believe that everything is fair game, from enhancing the colors to adding clouds from a different photo. I fall somewhere in between, with an overall objective of just trying to make a pretty picture.

IMPORTING MY IMAGES

If you recall way back in Chapter 1, we covered the import process. I have selected seven images for us to work with and put them in a folder, which we now need to import into the Elements Organizer for editing.

1. Choose File > Get Photos and Videos > From Files and Folders (**Figure 9.1**).

2. Navigate to the folder where the images are stored, press Control-A (Command-A) to select all, and click Open (**Figure 9.2**).

FIGURE 9.1
Import images into the Organizer.

FIGURE 9.2
Select all the images.

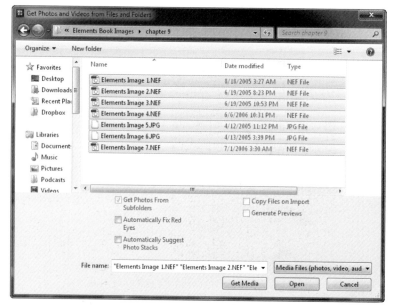

SIMPLE FIX

Let's start with one that just needs minor editing: Elements Image 5.jpg.

This photo doesn't need much, but the one thing that I want to change is the crop. The main subject is the hand, with all of its unique character. Let's get rid of the distractions by using the Crop tool.

1. Select the image, click the Fix tab, and then click Edit Photos.

2. When the file opens in the Editor, press the C key to select the Crop tool.

3. In the tool options bar above the image area, change the Aspect Ratio setting to Use Photo Ratio.

4. Draw out a crop around the hand and then rotate the crop window so that it is better oriented to the hand. Press Enter when done (**Figure 9.3**).

5. Add some sharpness by choosing Enhance > Unsharp Mask. Set the options to Amount 95, Radius 1, Threshold 5, and click OK (**Figure 9.4**),

6. Finally, go to the Filter menu and select Correct Camera Distortion. When the dialog opens, set Vignette to –100 and Midpoint to +19. Click OK (**Figure 9.5**).

FIGURE 9.3
Draw a crop around the hand.

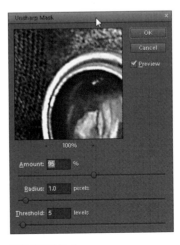

FIGURE 9.4
The Unsharp Mask sharpening settings.

FIGURE 9.5
Adding a vignette with the Camera Distortion tool.

GETTING RID OF THE HEADROOM

The next image we will work on, Elements Image 6.jpg, also needs a little help with the crop. The problem is that there is a little too much headroom, or empty space, over the subjects. To make this a more intimate image, we need to crop things a bit tighter.

FIGURE 9.6
Crop in tight to eliminate the headroom.

1. Select the image, click the Fix tab, and then click Edit Photos.

2. When the file opens in the Editor, press the C key to select the Crop tool.

3. Go to the tool options bar above the image area and change the Aspect Ratio setting to Use Photo Ratio.

4. Draw out a crop around the three figures and press the Enter key when done (**Figure 9.6**).

5. This image is suffering from color overload, but I think it would make a great black and white. Choose Enhance > Convert to Black and White.

6. Select the Portraits style and then click OK (**Figure 9.7**).

7. Finish off with some Unsharp Mask sharpening using the same settings as the last image.

FIGURE 9.7
Select Portraits from the black and white styles.

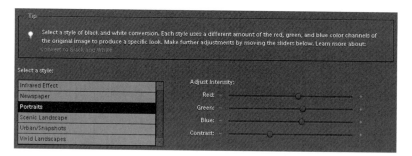

BLACK AND WHITE WITH A TINT

Since we just made one black and white image, why not continue with one more and use a slightly different effect? Select the file named Elements Image 2.NEF and send it to the Editor. Since this is a raw photo, we will need to do some work in Camera Raw first.

1. In the Camera Calibration tab, select the Camera Standard profile.

2. In the Detail tab, set the options to the following: Amount 90, Radius 1.0, Detail 25, and Masking 40 (**Figure 9.8**). There is no need to touch the Noise Reduction setting for this image.

3. In the Basic panel, use the settings Exposure –.35, Fill Light 10, Blacks 21, and Clarity +50. Click Open Image when done.

4. Choose Enhance > Convert to Black and White, and select the Infrared Effect style. Click OK to apply (**Figure 9.9**).

5. Click the Create New Adjustment Layer icon at the bottom of the Layers panel and select Photo Filter.

6. Choose Sepia from the Filter list and change the Density setting to 55% to finish off the effect (**Figure 9.10**).

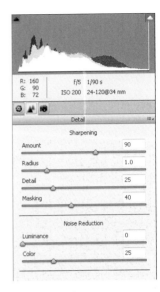

FIGURE 9.8
Making adjustments in the Detail panel.

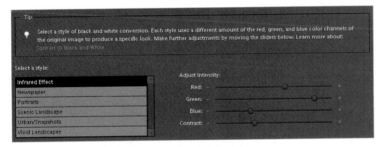

FIGURE 9.9
Select Infrared Effect.

FIGURE 9.10
Add a Sepia filter from the adjustment layers.

TAMING THE DUST SPOTS

If you are shooting with a digital SLR, you will have to deal with dust spots sooner or later. The perfect solution would be to clean your sensor before every photo shoot, but that's unrealistic. So let me show you how I deal with the dust spots that creep into my photos between camera cleanings.

1. In the Organizer, select Elements Image 3.NEF and open it in Camera Raw.

2. In the Camera Calibration panel, select the Camera Vivid profile.

3. In the Detail panel, set Amount to 85 and Masking to 60. Leave everything else set to the defaults.

4. Use the following settings in the Basic panel: White Balance Daylight, Exposure +.25, Recovery 100, Fill Light 10, Blacks 10, Brightness +45, Clarity +40, and Vibrance +10.

5. Click and hold the Crop tool, select an aspect ratio of 2 to 3, and draw out a tighter crop on the ornament (**Figure 9.11**).

FIGURE 9.11
Cropping with a 2 to 3 aspect ration.

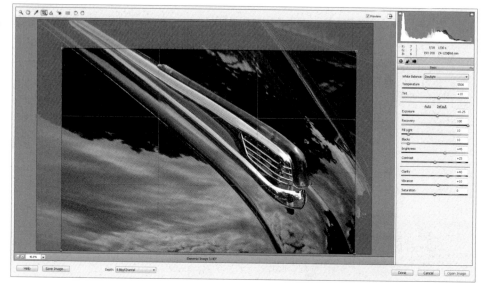

6. Open the image in the Editor, and press the J key to activate the Spot Healing Brush tool. Enlarge the image, use the bracket keys to make the brush just larger than the dust spots, and click the brush on the spots to eliminate them (**Figure 9.12**).

FIGURE 9.12
Click with the Spot Healing Brush to remove dust spots.

7. To quickly move through the image, hold down the spacebar to activate the Hand tool. Click and drag to a new location on the image and release the spacebar. Continue clicking on the dust spots until they are all gone.

8. Apply some Unsharp Mask sharpening to finish things off.

OPENING THE SHADOWS

This next image is kind of dark, which was intended, but I want more details in the shadow areas. Let's see what we can do with some Camera Raw adjustments.

1. In the Organizer, select Elements Image 1.NEF and open it in Camera Raw.

2. In the Camera Calibration panel, select the Camera Standard profile.

3. In the Detail panel, set Amount to 105 and Masking to 50.

4. In the Basic panel, change the Temperature setting to 3900 and the Tint setting to −21.

5. Move the Fill Light slider to 30 to open up the shadows, and move the Blacks setting to 10.

6. Move the Clarity slider to +100 to add lots of midtone contrast.

7. Use the Straighten tool to draw a line along the bottom of the engine and straighten up the crop (**Figure 9.13**).

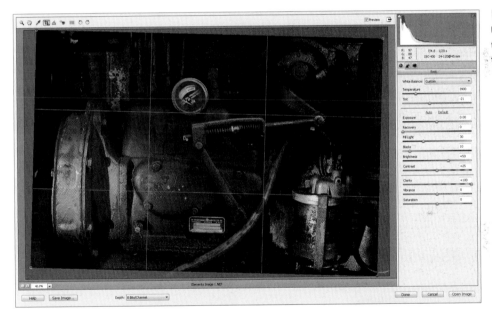

FIGURE 9.13
Use the Straighten tool to square things up.

8. Open the image in the Editor, and press Control-J (Command-J) to duplicate the layer.

9. Choose Filter > Other > High Pass, and set the Radius to 10.

10. Finally, set the blend mode to Soft Light (**Figure 9.14**).

FIGURE 9.14
Set the blend mode to Soft Light.

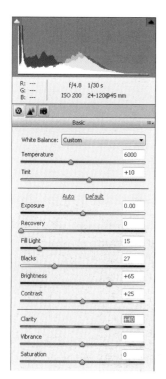

FIGURE 9.15
The settings in the Basic tab.

DARKENING THE EDGES

This next image really needs some help. It is kind of boring, partly because of the composition and partly because it lacks any real color vibrance.

1. In the Organizer, select Elements Image 4.NEF and open it in Camera Raw.

2. Press the L key to rotate the image counterclockwise.

3. Press the C key to activate the Crop tool and change the composition to something more appealing.

4. In the Camera Calibration panel, select the Camera Landscape profile.

5. In the Detail panel, set Amount to 90 and Masking to 48.

6. Change the White Balance setting to Cloudy and then adjust the Temperature to 6000.

7. Change Fill Light to 15, Blacks to 27, Brightness to +65, and Clarity to +40 (**Figure 9.15**). Open the image in the Editor.

8. Click the Create a New Layer icon and then press Alt-Backspace (Option-Delete) to fill it with black.

9. Press the M key for the Rectangular Marquee tool and then draw a selection inside the image edge, about a quarter-inch from the edge (**Figure 9.16**).

10. Choose Select > Feather, set the feather radius to 50, and press Enter. Press Delete to reveal the image below.

11. Press Control-D (Command-D) to remove the selection, and change the blend mode to Multiply.

FIGURE 9.16
Delete the selected portion of the black layer to add a nice edge effect.

THE PRE-DAWN LANDSCAPE FIX

This last file is from one of my favorite photo shoots. I drove for over an hour in the pitch black to arrive with my friends at the Monument Valley visitor's center, where we were greeted by some fantastic-looking light. Even though I took care to set my camera correctly, there are a lot of little things that need fixing in this image.

1. In the Organizer, select Elements Image 7.NEF, and open it in Camera Raw.

2. When Camera Raw opens, use the Straighten tool to draw a line along the horizon (**Figure 9.17**).

FIGURE 9.17
Adjusting for the
horizon line with
the Straighten tool.

3. In the Camera Calibration panel, select the Camera Landscape profile.

4. In the Basic panel, adjust the White Balance setting to Daylight.

5. Even though the image is dark, some areas of the sky are very bright, so reduce Exposure to −.45 and set the Recovery slider to 50.

6. To open up the shadows, move the Fill Light slider to 55, set Blacks to 15, and take the Brightness setting to +70.

7. To add some pop to the photo, set Clarity to +26 and Vibrance to +10.

8. Now that the details of the image are more visible, go to the Detail panel and set Amount to 85 and Masking to 55. Open the image.

9. To give the sky more contrast, select it with the Quick Selection tool, click the New Adjustment Layer icon, and select Levels (**Figure 9.18**).

10. In the Adjustments panel, set the black point to 20, the gray point to 0.84, and the white point to 240.

FIGURE 9.18
Add a Levels adjustment layer after selecting the sky to automatically mask out the ground.

Conclusion

There is nothing over the top or magical about these edits. They are just basic processes that, when applied correctly, can have a dramatic effect on an image. The most important part of image processing is being able to look at a photo and know what it needs to look better. This doesn't happen overnight. It takes time and practice to get really good at image editing, but the more you work at it the better you will become. And with all the skills and techniques that you learned in the last few chapters, you should be well on your way to producing stunning images.

Index

Reset button, 89
resizing. *See* sizing/resizing
rotation tools
    Camera Raw, 76
    Elements Editor, 93, 94

S

Saturation slider, 49, 69
Save As options, 90–92
Save Layers check box, 130
Screen blend mode, 121, 122
selecting photos, 21, 166
selections, 110–115
    copying/pasting, 114
    inverting, 114, 136
    keyboard shortcuts for, 114
    Lasso tools for, 111–112
    layer masks using, 119–120
    Magic Wand tool for, 112–113
    making masks from, 122
    Marquee tools for, 110–111
    protecting image areas with,
     109–110
    Quick Selection tool for, 52–53, 113
    refining edges of, 114–115
    tips for working with, 113–115
selective edits, 52–57, 105–123
Sepia filter, 169
shadows
    Fill Light slider for, 68
    opening details in, 171
    Quick fix of, 49
Shadows slider, 49
sharing photos, 156–159
    on Facebook, 158–159
    on Flickr, 156–158
sharpening images, 100
    Adjust Sharpness tool for, 101
    Auto Sharpen tool for, 43
    Camera Raw options for, 70–71
    High Pass filter for, 128
    for printing, 100, 146
    Quick Sharpen tool for, 50
    Unsharp Mask tool for, 102, 167
Show All button, 8, 27

showing your work, 143–161
    emailing photos, 159–160
    printing photos, 146–156
    sharing photos online, 156–159
Shutterfly, 154, 155
Single Photo view, 22, 31
sizing/resizing
    brushes, 52
    layers, 140
    prints, 147, 151
    thumbnails, 30
skies, 128–131
    darkening, 129–130
    gradients on, 130–131, 141
    Levels adjustment, 174
    quick fix of, 54–56
slideshows, 32, 33
Smart Albums, 25–27
Smart Fix slider, 48
Smart Tags, 20–21
social media sites, 156–159
Soft Light blend mode, 128, 131,
  132, 171
sorting images, 22–27
    creating albums for, 24–25
    Smart Albums for, 25–27
    star ratings for, 22–24
Spot Healing Brush tool, 108–109, 170
stacking images, 27–30, 35
    creating stacks, 28–29
    using suggested stacks, 29
star ratings, 22–24
Straighten tool, 74–75, 171, 173
subfolders, 6

T

tagging images. *See* keyword tags
teeth, whitening, 54
Text tool, 152
texture layer, 139–140
Threshold slider, 102
thumbnails
    keyword tag, 20
    sizing/resizing, 30
Tint slider, 50

Tolerance slider, 112
tonal adjustments
    Auto Levels option for, 42
    Exposure slider for, 66

U

underexposed photos, 67
Unsharp Mask tool, 102, 167

V

Vertical Perspective slider, 137–138
Vibrance slider, 69
viewing images, 30–33
    Film Strip view, 33
    Full Screen view, 31–33
    Show All button, 8, 27
    Single Photo view, 22, 31
    thumbnails view, 30
vignettes, 135–136

W

Weston, Edward, 131
White Balance settings, 66, 172
whitening teeth, 54
wide angle lenses, 137
Windows computers
    default printer settings on, 153
    keyboard shortcuts on, x
    opening Organizer on, 5
workflow, 163–175
    B&W tint, 169
    Camera Raw, 80
    dust spot removal, 170
    edge darkening, 172
    headroom crop, 168
    image import process, 166
    pre-dawn landscape fix, 173–174
    shadow lightening, 171
    simple fix, 167

Z

Zoom tool, 52, 73
zooming in/out, 32